Welcome TO OUR TABLE

SHIRLEY AND DANAE DOBSON
PHOTOGRAPHY BY JULIE JOHNSON

HARVEST HOUSE PUBLISHERS
EUGENE, OREGON

Welcome to Our Table

Text copyright © 2012 by Shirley Dobson and Danae Dobson
Photography copyright © 2012 by Julie Johnson, Vine Images

Published by Harvest House Publishers
Eugene, Oregon 97402
www.harvesthousepublishers.com

ISBN 978-0-7369-4389-5

Design and production by Garborg Design Works, Savage, Minnesota

Photo on page 19 used with permission from Kevin Still, Redhead Talent & Production, 626-257-3484, www.redheadtalent.com

All Scripture quotations, unless otherwise indicated, are taken from The Holy Bible, New International Version® NIV®. Copyright © 1973, 1978, 1984, 2011 by Biblica, Inc.™ Used by permission of Zondervan. All rights reserved worldwide. www.zondervan.com

Verses marked KJV are taken from the King James Version of the Bible.

Printed in China
12 13 14 15 16 17 18 19 20 / FC / 10 9 8 7 6 5 4 3 2 1

Contents

A Lost Art

THOUGHTS FROM SHIRLEY

My husband isn't likely to admit it to you, but he is a very good cook, that is when family or friends can get him into the kitchen. His specialties have become some of our favorites. One of those rare events occurred several weeks ago when a physician friend and his wife joined us for dinner along with two other couples. Jim prepared his wonderful Southern fried chicken. He didn't need a recipe because when he was a boy, his mother taught him all he needed to know. Unfortunately she didn't teach him how to keep things clean while he works. He absolutely destroys my kitchen when he fries. Let me set the scene for you on that special evening.

Jim was adorned with an apron, and the canola oil was popping all over the stove. Ingredients were strewn everywhere when our guests began to arrive. Jim was up to his elbows in flour, and he trailed it all the way to the front door. Everyone caught the spirit of the occasion and pitched in to help. We were all laughing and having such a good time. Then when everything was ready, we sat down for a marvelous meal of perfectly fried chicken, mashed potatoes and gravy, and all the trimmings. It was soul food at its best. We topped the meal off with apple pie and frozen yogurt. (No, Jim didn't bake the pie.) The best part of the evening was the warm fellowship we enjoyed, replete with stories and laughter. There is no restaurant anywhere that could have provided the pleasure and unique cuisine of this evening spent together.

I loved it because I have always cherished family, faith, and friends. I'm sure it is because as little girl, I didn't grow up in a loving environment. My father had a severe drinking problem, so when guests came by for a visit, we never knew if my father would show up and embarrass us. I knew very early in life that, above all else, I wanted to have a loving, stable home when I grew up. I also wanted to marry someone like Jim. As it turned out, I had to wait until college to meet him. Other than my relationship with Jesus Christ, Jim has been God's greatest blessing in my life.

I wanted a home that would reflect the values that mean so much to me. I am not a decorator, but I have an eye for beauty and charm. The houses we have lived in have not been large, but they have been expressions of my personality. Having friends join us here in our townhouse for times of hospitality and fellowship is such a pleasure to me. The Scripture teaches that it is fitting and proper for believers to welcome others into their homes. Here are some of the references:

- *Share with the Lord's people who are in need. Practice hospitality* (Romans 12:13).
- *A bishop then must be blameless, the husband of one wife, vigilant, sober, of good behaviour, given to hospitality, apt to teach* (1 Timothy 3:2 KJV).
- *...is well known for her good deeds, such as bringing up children, showing hospitality, washing the feet of the Lord's people, helping those in trouble and devoting herself to all kinds of good deeds* (1 Timothy 5:10).
- *Rather he must be hospitable, one who loves what is good, who is self-controlled, upright, holy and disciplined* (Titus 1:8).
- *Use hospitality one to another without grudging* (1 Peter 4:9 KJV).

These verses leave no question about the importance of being gracious to others by inviting them into our homes. In 3 John 8, it reads, "We ought therefore to show hospitality to such men so that we may work together for the truth." In short, being kind to others provides an opportunity to introduce the love of Jesus to those who might not know Him. That is not only relevant to adults, but it also applies to children.

I taught Bible stories for years to my kids and to other boys and girls in our neighborhood. Many of them gave their hearts to the Lord, and some, including my son and daughter, have gone on to serve Him diligently as adults.

But what about the art of hospitality? Both Danae and Ryan had a tendency to be messy when they were young, and I wondered if they were absorbing the principles on which home and family are built. During adolescence their rooms were often wrecked, and their clothes were scattered around. (Perhaps watching their father mess up the kitchen while frying chicken had a powerful influence on them.)

After Danae was grown and had a place of her own, I was delighted to see how she kept her apartment. I visited her one afternoon and found everything clean and in good order. I walked over to a curio cabinet that held porcelain animals and other artistic items. I leaned over to take a closer look, and Danae said firmly, "Mom, you are leaving finger prints on the glass!" *She gets it*, I thought with a secret smile.

I learned years later just how well the lessons of hospitality had taken root. When Jim and I reached our fiftieth wedding anniversary a year ago, our daughter planned and hosted an event to help us celebrate. Our son, Ryan, lived in another state, so he was not available to participate though he helped financially. It was an incredible affair. Danae selected lavender and yellow for the decor, which were the same colors I had chosen for our wedding. The flowers were purchased by Jim's publisher, Tyndale House, and were gorgeous. They were chosen by an artistic friend, arranged by a local florist, placed into pedestal vases, and set onto round tables. A string ensemble was engaged to play classical music throughout the evening, and every detail of the program was exquisitely planned. Danae asked a comedian to entertain the guests, and a scrumptious meal was provided. More than one hundred and seventy-five guests attended the event, which was held in the California church where we had been members for more than thirty years. The banquet room where we gathered looked like a wedding ceremony was about to begin. It was a wonderful evening, and I couldn't have been more proud of my precious son and daughter.

And now, as further evidence of Danae's early home life, she has asked me to co-author this book on Christian hospitality. It was her idea because, to my delight, she too loves family, faith, and friends.

We hope you enjoy the stories, photos, and recipes provided in the pages that follow. If you put them into practice, perhaps your grown daughter will someday implement them in her home. But be careful not to get your fingerprints on her glass cabinet.

THOUGHTS FROM DANAE

If there's one aspect of modern life that seems to be missing in our busy, fast-paced society, it's the provision of hospitality to our fellow travelers. We've become so weighed down by all the responsibilities and activities that we're dealing with that there's not much time left for friends. Meaningful interaction with others is hard to come by in this breathless world.

My parents have described an era from their childhoods that was less complicated. Back then it was typical for friends and relatives to drop by unexpectedly. My dad talks about the many times when he heard a knock on the screen door as someone called out, "Anybody home?" His mother would welcome the visitor with a cheerful, "Come on in!" and then hurry to put the coffeepot on the stove. After she served her guest some pie from the refrigerator, which was referred to as the icebox in those days, she and her visitor would sit in the living room and chat.

Those more casual days are gone now, or at least they're not as common. Twenty-first century life is not conducive to unexpected interruptions in the hustle and bustle of nonstop activity. Yet all around us, there are lonely people who desperately need contact and fellowship. Numerous souls are struggling personally or spiritually and may not even know why they're here.

It is for that purpose that my mother and I have written this book. Hospitality and expressions of human kindness are simply too important to be overlooked. Our objective is to provide ideas and illustrations to help you reach out to others in love and friendship. Whether you are serving a lavish meal with flowers and candles or whipping up a few refreshments for Bible study, God wants to use you (and your home) to minister to the needs of others. Your children will benefit too as they see you model what it means to exemplify the love of Christ.

I have to say that my mother is a class act when it comes to entertaining guests. I've seen her host everything from neighborhood get-togethers to formal luncheons for her National Day of Prayer Task Force. She's all about details! Each event is thoughtfully considered, and she always makes sure Christ is the unseen guest at every meal. Years ago she coauthored the book *Let's Make a Memory* with Gloria Gaither. In it she shared many of our family traditions that came from her creative mind. Yes, my mom is a veteran at hospitality, and I'm thrilled to have her contribute to this book. Can you tell I'm a proud daughter?

One of my favorite aspects of my mom's traditions is the delicious food she prepares in her kitchen. The majority of our holiday celebrations include certain recipes, some of which have been passed down for generations. Of course, having the sweet tooth that I do, the cakes and pies appeal the most to me. Not only do I like to eat them, but I enjoy preparing them too.

Baking has been a hobby of mine ever since my parents presented me with a battery-operated Easy-Bake Oven at the age of five. I remember staring into the orangey glow of that oven's plastic window and eagerly waiting for the chocolate cake to finish baking. It seemed to take forever!

As I grew older, I would come home from school and bake whatever I happened to be craving at the moment. My mom was not always happy to see her clean kitchen turned upside down when she got home. In fact she's never let me forget the time she discovered a Crisco smudge on her fabric-covered chair. Okay, so I got a little distracted by the television while baking cookies—it was a junior-high moment.

As the years went by, I became a savvy baker and occasionally surprised Mom with a three-layer cake, presented on a glass cake plate in a nice, clean kitchen. Eventually she even stopped checking her furniture for Crisco stains.

For me, food is associated with warm memories. I loved to watch my mom and her mother, Grandma Alma, prepare dishes for holidays and other special occasions. There was always a spirit of love and laughter, and I was fascinated by the stories they told from the past.

As I was going through my mom's recipe box for this book, I discovered handwritten cards that belonged to Grandma Alma, as well as Grandmother Myrna and Aunt Lela. Each was an accomplished cook and often worked their magic without recipes. They could tell if a substance was the right texture by how it felt. I'll never forget the time I was lying in bed listening to Aunt Lela rattling around in our kitchen. I got up to investigate, and there she was, surrounded by flour, preparing six pies and a pound cake. Not one recipe card was in sight!

As for me, I need instructions, and I'm glad I have them. Throughout these pages you will find some of those recipes along with uplifting stories, Scriptures, and attractive photos. My mom and I hope they will inspire you to live out the practice of hospitality (Romans 12). Don't let our busy world prevent you from making that a priority. Carve out some time to build relationships and strengthen your family by providing comfort, delicious food, and Christian fellowship. By doing so, you will bless people and bring glory and honor to your heavenly Father.

Spring

SPRING GARDEN DINNER FOR FRIENDS

THE BACKYARD BECOMES THE PERFECT BACKDROP FOR A LOVELY SPRING GARDEN DINNER.

A Fresh Start · *Danae*

As the days get warmer, the grass becomes greener, and the trees begin to bear fruit, my thoughts turn to the great outdoors. Some of my favorite activities of the season involve scouting nurseries for new plants and flowers and eating meals on the patio. When spring is in the air, it's like an open invitation to enjoy the beauty of God's creation.

Spring is also ideal for outdoor entertaining. When hosting evening get-togethers, it's fun to create ambiance with twinkle lights, candle lanterns, and fresh flowers. Seasonal foods are a delight to serve too! Colorful salads, fresh vegetables, and tangy strawberries are a reminder to guests that spring has sprung.

Why not take advantage of the warmer temperatures by hosting a garden dinner? You can create elegance by adding just a few special touches to your menu and decor. Delicious dishes and fragrant flowers set the perfect stage for a memorable evening.

When thinking through your guest list, you may want to consider inviting someone who doesn't know the Lord. So often we're tempted to spend all our time with fellow believers. That's understandable because it's refreshing to be in the company of those who share our faith. However, we can be effective witnesses for Christ by bringing nonbelievers into our homes to dine with us. Something significant occurs when we break bread together and experience love and communion around the table. It also provides an opportunity to engage in spiritual discussion. As you'll recall, Jesus used the "table talk" method throughout His ministry, and it resulted in life-changing decisions.

In addition to those who don't know the Lord, we all have Christian friends who are going through hardships. Right now you might be thinking of some people—or perhaps just one individual—who could be blessed by your good food and generous heart. There have been times when I've set the dining room table with fine china and candles and cooked a homemade dinner for a girlfriend who was going through a difficult time. It provided joy and a distraction for her.

Whomever God has laid on your heart, I hope you'll invite that person (or persons) over for a meal. Whether it's indoors or out, it's sure to be an encouragement to them—and to you!

Please send them on their way in a manner that honors God. 3 John 6

11

Since moving to Colorado Springs more than twenty years ago, God has blessed us with a new network of friends. Maybe you know a family who has recently moved to your neighborhood. Why not extend a warm welcome by inviting them for dinner or taking them a one-dish meal?

Chicken and Veggies in a Bag

- 1 whole chicken
- 1 sliced lemon
- Black pepper
- 4 medium potatoes, peeled and cut into large pieces
- 8 carrots, peeled and cut into large pieces
- 4 stalks celery, cut into large pieces
- 2 medium yellow onions, cut into fourths

Wash the chicken and pat dry. Sprinkle with ground pepper to taste. Place the sliced lemon inside the chicken cavity and then put the whole chicken into an oven bag. Add the vegetables.

Stir the following ingredients together well:

- 1 package dry onion soup mix
- 2 cups water
- 1 tablespoon cornstarch

Pour liquid over the chicken, seal the oven bag, and bake in a 350° oven for 1½ to 2 hours. Yield: 4-6 servings

Rose Garden · *Shirley*

Since my earliest childhood, I have loved flowers. I've been especially awed by the delicate beauty of roses. When Jim and I bought our first home in Southern California, I was determined to have a flower garden, but I wasn't very savvy about roses. Fortunately a friend knew all about them. She helped me plant twelve rosebushes and taught me how to prune them, where to cut the stems, and what they needed for nourishment. Through the years we lived in that little home, the garden provided beautiful, fresh-cut roses for our table.

As our family grew, we began to look for a larger home. Knowing I would have to leave my lovely rose garden, I prayed, *"Lord, You know how much I love these roses, and You say You want to give Your children the desires of their hearts. Could You find us a house with a few roses?"* I knew it was a presumptuous prayer in a world where millions of people don't have jobs or enough to eat each day, but I asked for this love gift nonetheless.

We soon found a cute home that was owned by an elderly couple needing to move away. The house fit our very limited budget, and we asked to see the property. The first time we toured the house, we were unable to look outside because it was night. When we decided it was the home for us, we went back during the day. There in the backyard were ninety-nine rosebushes of every color imaginable!

"Lord, You are so good!" I said as I raised my hands to Him. There we were surrounded by His magnificent creation.

We lived in that home for nineteen years, raised our children there, and made many happy memories with neighbors and relatives. Countless meals were cooked in my kitchen, and I enjoyed using the roses from my beautiful garden as centerpieces for my table. I loved to send bouquets home with people who needed their spirits lifted, and my roses brightened hospital rooms through the years. The Lord not only gave me the desire of my heart but allowed me to share that gift with others. When the flowers were in bloom, I enjoyed serving many meals in the beauty of our backyard.

Then as the years passed, the Lord called us to Colorado, and I had to let go. Moving is difficult, especially for a woman who is leaving behind many years of memories. But through the painful experience, my heavenly Father taught me an important lesson.

I missed Southern California and the college friends we had cultivated through the years. Colorado did not seem like home to me. I struggled with leaving my grown children, my aging parents, and even the home where my roses grew. Then one day when I was getting ready to leave for the office, I felt God speaking to me. He seemed to say, "Shirley, I'm not concerned about your happiness. I want you to be in the center of My will, and I have called you to Colorado for My purposes." He impressed upon me that I had been focusing on my own desires. And while He wants His children to enjoy His gifts—roses included—He wants most of all for us to conform to His will. Sometimes that means letting go and moving on.

From that day I knew without a doubt that Jim and I were right where God wanted us to be. No, we have no roses in Colorado Springs, but I have some wonderful memories of them.

Trust in the LORD with all your heart and lean not on your own understanding; in all your ways submit to him, and he will make your paths straight. PROVERBS 3:5-6

SOUTHERN SWEET TEA

6 black tea bags
2 cups water
⅛ teaspoon baking soda
1½ to 2 cups granulated sugar
6 cups cold water

Place tea bags and baking soda in a large glass measuring cup or ceramic teapot. (The baking soda softens the natural tannins that cause a bitter taste.) Boil the 2 cups water and then pour over the tea to form a concentrate. Cover and steep for 15 minutes. Remove tea bags (be careful not to squeeze them). Pour concentrate into a 2-quart pitcher and add sugar. Stir until dissolved. Add the cold water. Cool and serve with ice. Yield: 2 quarts

FINELY CHOPPED SPRING GREEN SALAD

1 small bunch green leaf lettuce

2 or 3 leaves green kale

2 bunches baby bok choy

4 to 6 small seedless cucumbers

2 avocados

⅓ of a 3-ounce package mint, stems removed

⅓ bundle of parsley, stems removed

½ cup cran raisins

½ cup garbanzo beans

⅓ cup green edamame beans

4-inch piece of fresh ginger

⅓ cup extra light olive oil

½ lemon

¼ cup orange blossom honey

Kosher salt to taste

The secret to this salad is finely chopping all the ingredients. Chop the lettuce, kale, bok choy, cucumbers, avocado, mint, and parsley very small. Layer the ingredients in the order listed above to create a mound in the bowl (don't toss). Add cran raisins,

garbanzo beans, and edamame beans. Peel the fresh ginger. Using a garlic press, squeeze the ginger, sprinkling the juice over the ingredients in the bowl. Pour olive oil and the juice from the lemon over salad. Toss. Add honey and kosher salt to taste and toss salad again right before serving.
Yield: 8 servings

PECAN CATFISH

6 (5- to 7-ounce) catfish fillets

3 cups pecan pieces

1 cup dried bread crumbs

1½ teaspoons salt, divided

1½ teaspoons ground black pepper, divided

1 cup all-purpose flour

3 eggs

½ cup milk

1 tablespoon seafood seasoning

¾ cup butter or margarine, melted

Trim fat from the catfish fillets and set aside. In a blender or food processor,

grind pecans, bread crumbs, ½ teaspoon salt, and ½ teaspoon pepper until fine. Pour into a shallow dish. In another shallow dish, combine flour, ½ teaspoon salt and ½ teaspoon black pepper. In a medium bowl, beat the eggs and milk together. Mix in remaining ½ teaspoon salt and ½ teaspoon pepper. Season catfish with seafood seasoning. Dredge in flour and dip in the egg mixture. Roll catfish in the pecan mixture. Preheat oven to 400°. Lightly cover the bottom of a large ovenproof skillet with melted butter or margarine. On medium heat, brown catfish on both sides in the butter. Transfer skillet with catfish to preheated oven and bake for 5 minutes. Yield: 8 servings

PECAN SPIKED RICE

- 2 tablespoons unsalted butter or margarine
- ½ cup yellow onion, finely chopped
- ¼ cup shallot, minced
- 1 teaspoon kosher salt
- 1 bay leaf
- 1 cup long-grain white rice, uncooked
- 2 cups hot chicken broth
- ¼ teaspoon freshly ground black pepper
- 1 cup pecan pieces, chopped and toasted

In a 1½-quart saucepan, melt butter over medium heat. Add onion, shallot, salt, and bay leaf. Cook for 4 or 5 minutes, stirring frequently to prevent browning. Add rice and continue to cook until the grains of rice are thoroughly heated. Stir in hot chicken broth and black pepper and bring to a simmer. Lower heat and cover pan. Cook for 18 to 20 minutes or until all liquid is absorbed. Stir in toasted pecans. Yield: 6 servings

GREEN BEANS WITH CARAMELIZED ONIONS

- 2 pounds fresh green beans
- 2 large sweet onions
- 3 tablespoons butter or margarine, divided
- 3 tablespoons light brown sugar
- 1½ tablespoons balsamic vinegar

Trim beans. Cook in boiling water (enough to cover) for 12

to 15 minutes or until tender. Drain and set aside. Cut onions into thin slices and then cut each slice in half. Melt 1 tablespoon butter in a large nonstick skillet over medium–high heat and add onion slices. Cook 8 to 10 minutes (do not stir). Continue cooking onion and stir frequently for 15 to 20 minutes or until golden. Reduce heat to medium and stir in remaining 2 tablespoons butter and brown sugar. Add green beans and cook 5 minutes or until thoroughly heated. Add vinegar and toss to coat the beans.
Yield: 8 servings

Warm Chocolate Cobbler with Ice Cream or Whipped Cream

    1¼ cups granulated sugar,
        divided
    1 cup all-purpose flour
    7 tablespoons unsweetened
        cocoa, divided
    2 teaspoons baking powder
    ¼ teaspoon salt
    ½ cup milk
    ⅓ cup butter, melted
    ½ teaspoon vanilla
    ½ cup firmly packed light
        brown sugar

    1½ cups hot water
    Vanilla ice-cream or
        whipped cream

Preheat oven to 350°. In a medium bowl, stir together ¾ cup sugar, flour, 3 tablespoons cocoa, baking powder, and salt. Stir in milk, butter, and vanilla. Mix until smooth. Pour batter into an ungreased 8–inch square glass baking pan. Stir together remaining ½ cup sugar, brown sugar, and remaining 4 tablespoons cocoa. Sprinkle cocoa mixture evenly over batter. Pour hot water over the top (do not stir). Bake 35 to 40 minutes or until center of cobbler is almost set. Let stand for 15 minutes. To serve, spoon into individual dessert dishes. The cobbler makes its own chocolate sauce in the bottom of the pan. Spoon some sauce over each serving. Top with vanilla ice cream or whipped cream.
Yield: 8 servings

BRIDAL SHOWER BRUNCH BUFFET

LOVE IS IN THE AIR! YOU'LL WANT TO OFFER GUESTS
AN ARRAY OF TEMPTING TIDBITS IN HONOR OF THE
HAPPY COUPLE AWAITING THEIR BIG DAY.

CELEBRATION OF LOVE · *Danae*

$\mathcal{I}$s there any day in a woman's life more significant than her wedding day? I can't think of anything that rivals it. There's the dress, the flowers, the cake, and—oh, yes!—that amazing, handsome guy with whom she's going to spend the rest of her life. Most girls dream about their future role as a wife and mommy long before their grooms ever come on the scene. I remember sitting in church with a girlfriend when we were both sixteen and reading a note she had just handed to me. On it she had listed the first and middle names of the six children she hoped to have. (Obviously her mind wasn't on the sermon.) It's interesting that after she met and married her husband, she eventually did wind up with six kids!

Given the significance of a wedding in a young woman's life, what a neat opportunity it is to throw a bridal shower for her to cherish for all time. When I've planned such an event, I've done so knowing that I'm not just providing an experience for the bride but for everyone else who will be there. Through the years I can recall showers that I've attended, and each one left a mark on my life. That's what I think about when planning any type of party. I want to give people a special memory to reflect upon.

I took that experience to an entirely new level recently when I gave my parents a fiftieth anniversary party. One hundred and seventy-five guests attended the celebration, which was held in the banquet room at my home church. Having not planned my wedding (yet!), it was uncharted territory for me, and I really had to pray my way through the process. But the Lord caused the pieces to fall into place, and the party turned out to be "some enchanted evening." My brother, Ryan, and I set out to honor our parents for their faithfulness to God and to each other, and I think we accomplished that. Mom and Dad felt loved and appreciated.

Fifty years ago, when my mom's bridal shower took place, my dad was by her side (per her request). From time to time, he has remarked that he felt awkward sitting there, oohing and aahing over home decorating items and kitchenware. I think he would

Jim and Shirley cutting the cake at their fiftieth wedding anniversary celebration, August 28, 2010

have preferred to be elsewhere, eating a burger and watching a USC football game. In the modern day, it's become common for grooms to attend bridal showers, but it's my opinion that most would prefer to shy away from these "hen gatherings."

As women we are in our element at a bridal shower. The tasty treats, the games, the decorative gifts—we love them all! But the true essence of the event is keeping the Lord at the center. When I've hosted a bridal shower, I've planned a time to give the women an opportunity to offer prayers of blessing for the bride-to-be and also for her fiancé. What better way to send a couple off on one of the most significant experiences of their lives than bathing their relationship in prayer.

As my mom often says, "After a honeymoon comes a marriage." The couple will come home to bills, laundry, marital adjustments, and work, work, work! The challenges encountered can be overwhelming. Friends and family members must remember to pray for the newlyweds during their early years as husband and wife. Ask the Lord to draw them closer to Him and to bless their home and family as the years unfold.

A newly married couple must be absolutely committed to a lifetime love. If they're determined to make it work, and if they keep the Lord at the center of their union, perhaps they will celebrate their golden anniversary someday, just as my parents have done.

Love never fails. 1 CORINTHIANS 13:8

BRIDAL BRUNCH

Separate table for plates and napkins.

SET UP
- Bud vase with yellow roses
- Wedding announcement on stand
- Pink napkins tied with yellow ribbons, silver tied into napkins, stacked on a silver tray
- Stacked plates

Pick up napkin and plate and then come to the bridal buffet table for food and beverage.

BRIDAL BRUNCH TABLE

Flowers or fruit could substitute for centerpiece

Cups

Punch Orange Apricot

Tray

silver tray

Stacked doilies

Quiche Lorraine

could use round dish too

Pineapple shells filled with pineapple chunks

Honeydew shell filled with melon balls

silver tray

Sliced cantelope

crystal bowl

Bananas cut into large chunks. Roll in yogurt then in toasted coconut until well coated.

Coffee Cake

Pastries or Cinnamon Rolls

silver tray

Coffee

Tea

Cream   Sugar

Saucers

Stacked doilies

Stacked Cups

Tropical Banana Delight

4 sliced bananas
4 (6-ounce containers) vanilla yogurt,
    sweeten to taste with powdered
    sugar
Toasted coconut

In a medium bowl, lightly toss bananas in the yogurt mixture. Roll individual pieces in toasted coconut.
Yield: 8 servings

Quiche Lorraine

Pastry for a 9-inch one crust pie
8 slices bacon, crisply cooked
    and crumbled
1 cup (4 ounces) shredded natural
    Swiss cheese

⅓ cup finely chopped onion
4 eggs
2 cups heavy whipping cream
¼ teaspoon salt
¼ teaspoon black pepper
⅛ teaspoon ground red cayenne

Heat oven to 425°. Prepare pastry and ease into quiche dish or pie plate. Sprinkle bacon, cheese, and onion on pastry. Beat eggs slightly and then beat in the remaining ingredients. Pour into quiche dish. Bake for 15 minutes. Reduce oven temperature to 300° and bake approximately 30 minutes longer or until knife inserted in the center comes out clean. Let stand 10 minutes before cutting.
Yield: 6 servings

CINNAMON SOUR CREAM COFFEE CAKE

1 cup (½ pound) butter or margarine
1¼ cups granulated sugar
2 eggs
1 cup sour cream
2 cups flour
½ teaspoon baking soda
1½ teaspoons baking powder
1 teaspoon vanilla
Cinnamon nut mixture:
    ¾ cup finely chopped walnuts
    1 teaspoon cinnamon
    2 tablespoons granulated sugar

In a large bowl combine butter, sugar, and eggs. Beat until mixture is light and fluffy. Blend in sour cream. Sift flour, baking soda, and baking powder into the creamed mixture. Add vanilla. Blend well. Spoon half of the batter into a 9-inch greased tube pan (batter will be thick). Sprinkle half of the cinnamon nut mixture over batter. Spoon in remaining batter and top with remaining cinnamon nut mixture. Place in a cold oven. Set temperature to 350° and bake approximately 55 minutes. Cut slices in pan to serve warm or cool.
Yield: 8 to 10 servings

ORANGE PECAN ROLLS

1 package active dry yeast
¼ cup warm water
¼ cup granulated sugar
4 tablespoons (½ stick) butter or
    solid vegetable shortening
1¼ teaspoons salt
¾ cup boiling water
1 egg slightly beaten
3 to 3½ cups all-purpose flour

ICING

1½ cups powdered sugar
3 tablespoons butter, melted
½ teaspoon finely shredded orange peel
1 to 2 tablespoons orange juice
Chopped pecans for garnish

In a small bowl, dissolve yeast in the ¼ cup warm water. In a large bowl, combine granulated sugar, butter, and salt. Add the boiling water, stirring to dissolve sugar and melt butter. Let stand until temperature is 105° to 115°. Stir in the yeast mixture, egg, and 1½ cups flour. With a wooden spoon, beat until a smooth dough forms. Stir in another 1½ cups flour. Gradually stir in enough of the remaining flour to make a dough that pulls from the sides of the bowl (dough will be soft). Transfer to a greased bowl, turning the dough once to grease surface. Cover with plastic wrap and refrigerate for 2 to 24 hours.

To make the icing, combine the powdered sugar, melted butter, and orange peel in a medium bowl. Blend in enough orange juice to make the mixture easy to spread. Cover.

Punch dough down, cover, and let rest for 10 minutes. Using muffin pans, grease 18 cups. On lightly floured surface, roll dough into a 12 x 8-inch rectangle. Spread half of the icing to within ½ inch of edges. Cover remaining icing and set aside. Starting with a long side, roll dough into a spiral. Moisten the stem, and pinch the stem to seal. Using a sharp knife, cut into 18 slices. Place slices cut sides down in prepared muffin cups. Cover and let rise in a warm place until nearly doubled in size (approximately 30 minutes). Heat oven to 350°. Bake uncovered for 18 to 20 minutes or until golden brown. Remove rolls and place on wire racks. Cool slightly. Spread with remaining icing and sprinkle with chopped pecans. Serve warm.
Yield: 18 standard or 12 jumbo rolls

WHITE CHOCOLATE-DIPPED STRAWBERRIES

    18 to 24 large strawberries with leaves
    1 (12-ounce) bag white baking chips
    1 tablespoon shortening
    ½ cup semisweet chocolate chips
    1 teaspoon shortening

Cover a cookie sheet with waxed paper. Rinse strawberries and pat dry. Heat the white baking chips and 1 tablespoon shortening in a saucepan over low heat, stirring constantly until the chips are melted. Poke a fork into the stem end of each strawberry and dip three-fourths of the way into the melted chips, leaving the top of the strawberry and leaves uncoated. Place dipped strawberries on the waxed paper-covered cookie sheet. Heat the semisweet chocolate chips and 1 teaspoon shortening in another small saucepan over low heat, stirring constantly until chocolate chips are melted. Drizzle melted chocolate chips over the dipped strawberries, using a small spoon. Refrigerate uncovered approximately 30 minutes until coating is set.
Yield: 18 to 24 strawberries

ORANGE APRICOT REFRESHER

    1 quart orange juice
    1 quart apricot nectar
    Orange slices and halved strawberries
        for garnish

Combine orange juice and apricot nectar and chill. Serve in a punch bowl with orange slices and strawberries (halved and bottom side up). To serve more people, increase quantities in equal amounts.
Yield: 8 servings

Lazy Weekend Breakfast

Enjoy a leisurely weekend by inviting the special people in your life to join you for breakfast and devotions.

A Visit with a Friend · *Shirley*

When I was a sophomore in college, my friend Anita Wooten invited me to visit her parents' home one weekend. In the morning I awoke to the aroma of a wonderful breakfast of scrambled eggs, bacon, juice, and the best apple muffins I had ever tasted. But as delicious as the breakfast was, something even more significant happened. I remember it vividly to this day.

Anita's father, Mr. Wooten, bowed his head and thanked God for the food we were about to eat. I had never seen a family do that before. Then after we had finished the meal, he opened the Bible and read a passage to us. Finally this godly man asked each of us to kneel by our chairs and pray together. I learned later that this was a weekly event in their family. Every Saturday the entire family gathered to eat Mrs. Wooten's great breakfast, and then they took a few minutes to worship and pray.

Growing up in a home where faith was only nominal and God was far removed from daily life, I'd never witnessed anything like that. Our family never prayed together, not even at meals, and we certainly never read the Bible. Breakfast at the Wooten's house opened my eyes to how families could share more than a meal—they could enjoy spiritual nourishment together too.

The impact of this experience was profound. I saw how strong, loving Christian families incorporated their faith into their lives together. I decided on that morning that if the Lord allowed me to have a husband and children someday, we would kneel and pray together. And we have.

Anita and her family are still my good friends, and her mother's apple muffin recipe is now one of our family's traditions. I often bake them on special occasions. As the aroma rises from the oven, I remember my first weekend with this good, godly family.

Today we should look for opportunities to bring our children's and grandchildren's friends into our homes to model how prayer and our Christian faith are part of our daily experience. They and their families are watching us, and some of them will remember those moments for a lifetime.

Let your light shine before others, that they may see your good deeds and glorify your Father in heaven. Matthew 5:16

EASY BREAKFAST CASSEROLE

1 pound breakfast sausage,
    browned and drained
½ cup chopped green onions
½ cup chopped green peppers
1 (7-ounce) can sliced mushrooms or
    ½ cup freshly sliced mushrooms
1 (4-ounce) can mild green chilies
2 cups cheddar or Swiss cheese,
    shredded
8 eggs
3 cups milk
1½ cups premixed baking or biscuit mix

Lightly grease a 9 x 13-inch glass baking dish, place sausage in bottom of pan, and top with onions, green peppers, mushrooms, chilies, and cheese in that order. Beat together the eggs, milk, and premixed baking or biscuit mix. Pour egg mixture over meat mixture and bake at 375° for 45 minutes or until medium brown on top. Cool 20 minutes before serving.
Yield: 8 servings

Apple Muffins

1 cup apples, pare and cut apples into
  ¼-inch slices and then chop
¼ cup sugar
1 egg, well-beaten
⅔ cup low-fat milk
¼ cup butter or margarine
2 cups all-purpose flour
½ teaspoon salt
½ teaspoon cinnamon
¼ cup sugar
4 teaspoons baking powder

Topping

4 tablespoons butter or margarine,
  slightly softened
3 tablespoons sugar
1 tablespoon cinnamon

*In a large bowl, mix chopped apples and
¼ cup sugar. Blend in egg. Add milk and
butter. Mix lightly. Sift in dry ingredients
and mix well (batter will be thick). Spoon
into greased muffin tins. In a separate
bowl, mix topping. Spoon over each
muffin. Bake for 20 minutes at 350°.
Yield: 12 muffins*

EASTER

EASTER MEMORIES · *Shirley*

My mother was the glue that held our family together. If anything fun happened, it was because she was responsible for it. She was employed full-time, and yet she tried to make the holidays as special as she could for my brother and me. As for my dad, he was an absentee father who was rarely there for us.

One of my favorite days of the year was Easter, when winter was behind us and spring had arrived at last. The flowers were in bloom, and baby birds were chirping in their nests. I would peek in and watch them spreading their little wings and preparing for their first solo flights. I was also excited because the coming of Easter meant getting a new dress, gloves, and of course, a beautiful new hat. I would feel so pretty walking into church on that morning and thinking that every eye was on me. The lyrics of a song said it best: "I enjoy being a girl."

As you can discern from this description, at home I was not taught the real meaning of Easter. Then one day my mother encouraged us to attend a little evangelical church in our neighborhood, and it was there that I was taught who Jesus was. I learned that He died on a cruel cross for my sins, that He rose on the third day, and if I would put my trust in Him, I would have eternal life in heaven. Afterward I had an entirely different understanding of Easter. In fact, in my church it was appropriately called "Resurrection Day."

This beautiful china once belonged to Jim Dobson's maternal grandmother

When I had my own children, I didn't want them to confuse the fun of this holiday with the celebration of Jesus' death and resurrection. Therefore, I came up with the idea of "Easter Saturday." We dyed eggs on Friday night, and Jim hid them around the yard. We placed little stuffed bunnies in strategic places and gave the children baskets containing colorful candies. Then the children searched for the "treasure egg," which was bigger and silver in color. It was always harder to find. Inside it was a small amount of money, candy, or a toy. The finder of the treasure egg would always jump for joy.

The next morning our family went to church to learn about Jesus' resurrection and to sing together the old hymn.

Low in the Grave He Lay

Low in the grave He lay, Jesus my Savior,
Waiting the coming day, Jesus my Lord!

Up from the grave He arose,
With a mighty triumph o'er His foes,
He arose a victor from the dark domain,
And He lives forever, with His saints to reign.
He arose! He arose!
Hallelujah! Christ arose!

After the service we would invite family and friends to our table for a relaxed, traditional dinner of ham, twice-baked potatoes, warm rolls, vegetables, and molded salad. We topped it all off with strawberry cake and ice cream. What a treat!

My children are grown now, but I have wonderful warm memories of Easters past with my family. And on this special day they can be found in church, celebrating the death and resurrection of our Savior.

He is not here; he has risen! Luke 24:6

Pictured above is our son, Ryan Dobson, daughter-in-love, Laura, and grandson, Lincoln. Recently a new addition has been added to the Ryan Dobson household—a baby girl, Luci Rose. They live near Jim and me in Colorado Springs. Ryan and Laura are very generous and love to open their home to others. It is a family characteristic.

Menu

Ham with Raisin Sauce
Twice-Baked Potatoes
Rolls
Sautéed Spring Vegetables
Razzle-Dazzle Molded Jell-O Salad
Strawberry Cake

RAISIN SAUCE

1 cup raisins
2 cups water
2 tablespoons cornstarch
2 tablespoons granulated sugar
1/8 teaspoon salt
2 tablespoons cold water
1 tablespoon butter or margarine
2 tablespoons lemon juice

Simmer raisins in 2 cups water for 15 minutes. In a small bowl, combine cornstarch, sugar, salt, and cold water to make a paste. Add to raisins. Heat until thick. Remove from heat. Add butter or margarine and lemon juice. Mix well. Delicious on ham or roast pork.
Yield: 6 to 8 servings

SAUTÉED SPRING VEGETABLES

4 large carrots, peeled and cut into
    1/4-inch strips
3 tablespoons butter or margarine
1 tablespoon olive oil
3 (8-ounce) bags fresh sugar snap peas
2 yellow bell peppers, seeded and cut
    into 1/4-inch strips
2 teaspoons minced garlic
3/4 teaspoon salt
1/2 teaspoon ground black pepper

In a small saucepan of boiling water, blanch carrots for 2 minutes. Drain and set aside. In a large skillet, heat butter or margarine and olive oil over medium-high heat until butter melts. Add sugar snap peas, bell peppers, carrots, garlic, salt, and pepper. Cook for 4 to 5 minutes, stirring frequently until crisp-tender.
Yield: 8 servings

STRAWBERRY CAKE

1 white cake mix
1 cup oil
1 small box strawberry gelatin
½ cup cold water
4 eggs
1 small box or tub frozen
　　strawberries, thawed
3 tablespoons flour

ICING

1 (1-pound) box powdered sugar
½ teaspoon vanilla
¼ cup butter or margarine
Strawberries and juice to desired
　　consistency

Dissolve strawberry gelatin in cold water. In a large bowl, combine cake mix, oil, dissolved strawberry gelatin, eggs, ½ cup strawberries (with juice), and flour. Using electric mixer, blend ingredients at medium speed until smooth (approximately 5 minutes). Grease and flour a 9 x 13–inch pan or 2 layer pans. Pour batter into prepared pan(s) and bake at 350° for approximately 30 minutes. (If a toothpick inserted into the center of the cake comes out clean, it is done.)

To make icing combine powdered sugar, vanilla, and butter or margarine in a medium bowl. Add ¼ cup strawberries with juice and begin mixing with electric mixer. Continue adding strawberries and juice gradually until you reach desired consistency.
Yield: 10 or more servings

RAZZLE-DAZZLE MOLDED JELL-O SALAD

1 (6-ounce) package raspberry Jell-O
1 pint raspberry sherbet
1 tablespoon fresh lemon juice
1 (16-ounce) can smooth cranberry
　　sauce
1½ cups water

Boil water and then remove from heat. Add raspberry Jell-O. Stir until dissolved. Add lemon juice and raspberry sherbet. Mix well. Mash cranberry sauce. Fold into Jell-O mixture. Spray a 5-quart ring mold with no-stick cooking spray. Pour Jell-O mixture into the mold and chill to set.
Yield: 8 to 10 servings

SUMMER FORMAL TEA

TAKE TIME TO ENJOY A MEMORABLE SUMMER AFTERNOON, SIPPING TEA AND BONDING WITH THE GIRLS.

SWEET MEMORIES OF TEA · *Danae*

Don't you just love tea parties? There's something appealing about slipping on a pretty dress and getting together with friends over a piping hot pot of Earl Grey or almond spice tea. Then there's the delicious treats that go with the tea—the cucumber sandwiches, the flaky scones with raspberry jam and fresh cream, the fruit tarts and lemon squares. (Are you hungry yet?)

Taking tea, and with our pinkies up!

My mom instilled in me a love for tea parties, which date back to my early childhood. When I was a toddler, we celebrated rainy days by hosting these events for my stuffed animals. We'd set my little table with plastic china while listening to favorite Shirley Temple tunes. When I was five, my furry friends were replaced by real live guests as Mom and I started hosting elaborate tea parties for some children in our neighborhood. Our make-believe names, originated by none other than yours truly, were Mrs. Perry (me), Mrs. Green, Mrs. White, and Mr. Brown. I had the privilege of naming my mother as well and gave her the dignified title of Mrs. Snail. (We had a slight problem with snails in our rose bushes, so that was a common word in my five-year-old vocabulary.) My mom was a good sport about it and accepted the name Mrs. Snail with grace. In fact, she now has a small collection of crystal snails in her living room to which I've contributed.

Our neighborhood tea parties were so much fun, and they provided an opportunity to teach manners and etiquette, such as how to arrange silverware, hold and drink from a teacup, use a napkin, chew with mouths closed, and carry on a conversation. Our tea gatherings were an effective method of teaching common politeness, and my friends and I enjoyed acting out the instruction. My mom also used those opportunities to demonstrate how to pray before eating, and she explained why we paused to thank God for our food.

Through the years my mother and I have continued hosting tea parties for special friends and using those occasions to focus on the Lord in a significant way. We make a point of sharing what God is doing in our lives, discussing

PARENTING TIP:
My friend has four daughters, and as each girl turns thirteen, their mother gives them a "Blessing Tea." It involves not only inviting her daughter's 'tween friends but older women as well, who serve as mentors and role models. These women provide spiritual insight and advice and gather around the birthday girl to pray over her. They also encourage her to remain pure. A Blessing Tea is a great way to help launch a thirteen-year-old girl into adulthood.

our challenges, and praying for one another. It's a special and unique time of bonding. There's something about a party that includes women and teacups that seems to promote closeness and intimacy in a way that other social gatherings can't. Perhaps it stems from the fact that tea is a tradition that women have been engaging in to connect with one another for centuries. Or maybe it has to do with the absence of men. Whatever the reason, if you provide a table of women with a hot pot of tea, fancy teacups, and some goodies to munch on, you have the perfect setting for female bonding.

There's also a lot of laughter that takes place at these gatherings, especially once the cameras start clicking. One of my mom's favorite poses is to have all the ladies hold their teacups high, pinkie fingers extended. And if there happen to be formal hats, gloves, and fur wraps on hand, so much the better!

From what I've observed, there is an ongoing appreciation for tea that never diminishes. Women of all ages enjoy engaging in meaningful conversation with friends around a table enhanced by lovely flowers and china. What a beautiful setting to discuss our faith in Christ and encourage one another!

A friend loves at all times.
PROVERBS 17:17

36

Strawberry Salad with Cinnamon Vinaigrette
Scones with Raspberry Preserves, Lemon Curd, and Fresh Whipped Cream
  or Devonshire Cream
Heart-Shaped Tuna Sandwiches
Round Wheat Crackers with Strawberries, Cucumbers, and Watercress
Zucchini Bread and Cream Cheese Sandwiches
High Tea Vanilla Cookies • Mini Chocolate Cheesecakes • Luscious Lemon
  Cream Pie • Apricot Ginger Tea • Earl Gray Decaffeinated Tea

STRAWBERRY SALAD WITH CINNAMON VINAIGRETTE

1 (11-ounce) can mandarin oranges,
  drained
1 pint fresh strawberries, stemmed
  and halved
1 small red onion, thinly sliced
½ cup coarsely chopped pecans,
  toasted
1 avocado, cut into chunks
1 (10-ounce) package romaine
  lettuce

CINNAMON VINAIGRETTE

⅓ cup olive oil
⅓ cup raspberry vinegar
1 tablespoon sugar
½ teaspoon salt
½ teaspoon ground cinnamon
¼ teaspoon pepper
½ teaspoon hot sauce

To make cinnamon vinaigrette, combine all ingredients in a jar and shake vigorously. Cover and chill at least 2 hours. Shake well before serving.
Yield: ⅔ cup

To make salad, combine first 6 ingredients in a large bowl. Drizzle with half of the cinnamon vinaigrette and toss to coat. Serve remaining vinaigrette with the salad.
Yield: 6 servings

SCONES

⅓ cup butter or margarine
1¾ cups all-purpose flour
3 tablespoons sugar
2½ teaspoons baking powder
¼ teaspoon salt
1 egg, beaten
½ cup currants (optional)
4 to 6 tablespoons half-and-half
1 egg, beaten

Heat oven to 400°. Cut butter into flour, sugar, baking powder, and salt with pastry blender until mixture resembles fine crumbs. Stir in 1 beaten egg, the currants, and just enough half-and-half so dough leaves the sides of the bowl. Turn dough onto lightly floured surface. Knead lightly 10 times. Roll out dough to ½-inch thick and cut with a floured biscuit cutter. Place on ungreased cookie sheet. Brush dough with one beaten egg. Bake 10 to 12 minutes or until golden brown. Immediately remove from cookie sheet and cool slightly. Split scones. Spread with butter and serve with preserves and fresh whipped cream or Devonshire cream.
Yield: Approximately 15 scones

HEART-SHAPED TUNA SANDWICHES

2 (5-ounce) cans solid white tuna in
    spring water, drained and flaked
Mayonnaise
1 small red apple, peeled and diced
1 stalk celery, finely chopped
¼ cup finely chopped pecans,
16 slices wheat bread
Mango chutney

*Mix tuna and mayonnaise to desired
consistency. Add apple pieces, chopped
celery, and chopped pecans and mix
thoroughly. Using a large, heart-shaped
cookie cutter, cut heart shapes out of
the center of each slice of bread. Spread
light layers of mango chutney and tuna
mixture on each heart shape. Top with
another heart. Wrap a thin, pink satin
ribbon around each sandwich and tie
with a bow.*
Yield: 8 sandwiches

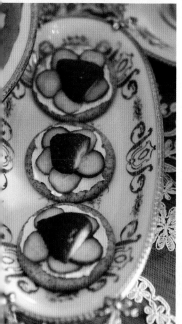

ROUND WHEAT CRACKERS WITH STRAWBERRIES, CUCUMBERS, AND WATERCRESS

4 ounces cream cheese, softened
1 tablespoon orange marmalade
½ cup fresh watercress, coarsely
    chopped
1 large cucumber, thinly sliced into
    18 circles
9 medium fresh strawberries
18 (2 to 2½-inch) round wheat
    crackers
Fresh sprigs of watercress for
    garnish

*In a small bowl, combine cream cheese,
marmalade, and chopped watercress
and mix well. Cut each strawberry in
half lengthwise. Just before serving,
spread cheese mixture on each cracker.
Top with a cucumber slice and another
layer of the cheese mixture. Place a
strawberry half (cut side down) on top
of the cheese mixture and gently press
down. Garnish each with a sprig of
watercress.*
Yield: 18 crackers

MINI CHOCOLATE CHEESECAKES

9 creme-filled chocolate
    sandwich cookies
2 (8-ounce) packages and
    1 (3-ounce) package cream
    cheese, softened
1 cup granulated sugar
¼ cup unsweetened cocoa powder
2 teaspoons vanilla extract
3 eggs
Fresh whipped cream and cookie
    pieces for garnish

*Heat oven to 350°. Line 18 medium
muffin cups with paper baking cups.
Split sandwich cookies in half. Place 1
cookie half, crème center side up, in each
cup. Beat cream cheese in a large bowl
with electric mixer on medium speed
until smooth. Gradually beat in sugar
and cocoa until fluffy. Beat in vanilla.
Beat in eggs one at a time until well
blended. Divide evenly into cups (cups
should be almost full). Bake 20 to
25 minutes or until centers are firm.
Cool 15 minutes. (Cheesecake centers*

will sink while cooling.) Refrigerate in muffin cups at least 1 hour. Cover and refrigerate 1 hour longer before serving. Place a dollop of whipped cream and a wedge of a chocolate sandwich cookie on each cheesecake. Serve immediately. Refrigerate remaining cheesecakes.
Yield: 18 servings

High Tea Vanilla Cookies

    2 cups butter at room temperature
        (it is very important that the
        butter is not softened or melted)
    ⅔ cup powdered sugar
    ½ teaspoon vanilla extract
    2 cups all-purpose flour
    1½ cups cornstarch

Vanilla Icing

    ⅓ cup butter at room temperature
    4 cups powdered sugar
    ½ teaspoon vanilla extract
    ⅓ cup milk

Preheat oven to 350°. In a large bowl, beat butter until creamy. Add powdered sugar and mix until light and fluffy. Add vanilla extract and beat well. Sift flour and cornstarch into butter mixture and beat until well mixed. Roll cookie dough into 1-inch balls. Place onto ungreased cookie sheets and bake 15 minutes or until bottoms are light brown. Carefully remove the cookies from the pan and cool on wire racks. (When warm, the cookies are delicate.)

To make vanilla icing, combine butter, powdered sugar, vanilla, and milk in medium bowl. Stir until well mixed.

When cookies are cool, spread with vanilla frosting.
Yield: 60 cookies

Luscious Lemon Cream Pie

    4 eggs, separated
    ½ cup sugar
    Grated peel and juice of 1 large
        lemon
    2 cups whipped cream
    Meringue crust
    1 tablespoon powdered sugar

Meringue Crust

    4 egg whites
    1 cup granulated sugar
    1 teaspoon lemon juice

To make meringue crust, beat egg whites until soft peaks form. Gradually add sugar, beating until stiff but not dry. Blend in lemon juice. Generously grease one 9-inch pie pan. Spoon meringue mixture into the pan. With a spoon push mixture up around edges to form a pie shell. Bake at 200° for 2 hours. Cool thoroughly before adding pie filling.

For filling, beat egg yolks with sugar, lemon peel, and juice until light. Pour into a double boiler and cook over simmering water until mixture is thick. Remove from heat and cool thoroughly. Fold in half of whipped cream. Turn into cooled meringue crust and refrigerate at least 2 hours to set. Fold powdered sugar into remaining whipped cream. Spread over chilled pie.
Yield: 1 (9-inch) pie

CHILDREN'S BIRTHDAY PARTY

WISHES ARE SURE TO COME
TRUE WITH A FUN AND
FESTIVE BIRTHDAY BASH.

A Day to Remember · *Danae*

The proud birthday girl on her new bicycle

Can you recall a significant birthday from your childhood? When you close your eyes, can you picture the people who were there and perhaps a special gift that made you smile?

My sixth birthday is one that I'll always cherish. My parents threw a party for me and invited both sets of grandparents, a few cousins, and special friends from school and church. I remember opening gifts and being flattered that one girl mistakenly gave me a "Happy Seventh Birthday" card. The Malibu Barbie doll was also a welcomed surprise. After I opened my presents and before we played games, everyone enjoyed lunch and cake on the picnic tables in our backyard. It was an exciting day for this wide-eyed child, but the best part occurred after my friends departed. My dad wheeled a new bicycle, complete with a white basket with pink and yellow plastic flowers, down the driveway. It was my own big-girl bike. I was overjoyed! That afternoon as the setting sun cast its golden hues on our neighborhood, I proudly peddled to my friend Suzanne's house to show her my new wheels. As I walked up her front porch steps and reached for the doorbell, I thought to myself, *I am six years old, and I will always remember this day.*

A birthday is significant in a child's life; therefore, it should be given high priority. The details and special touches that you put into making the occasion memorable will please your youngster and also the other children who attend. You can create an experience for them to last a lifetime. It doesn't have to be elaborate or cost a bundle. Children are easily amused. If you have an enticing theme, a few props, yummy food, and some stimulating games, you have all you need for a party extravaganza.

One thing is worth noting. Although a birthday party is a happy occasion for a child, it can be painful for a youngster who isn't invited. I remember experiencing that rejection one year. I was sitting in the backseat with two girls in my carpool, hearing them talk excitedly about their upcoming sleepover and their plans to watch *The Wizard of Oz.* For two weeks as we rode to and from school, they chatted about their anticipated evening, completely oblivious to my feelings. I didn't shed a

PARENTING TIP:
My mom threw birthday parties for my brother and me every other year. My parties occurred on even number years, such as four, six, and eight. Ryan's parties were held on his odd numbers, such as five, seven, and nine. By scheduling in this way, my mom only had to give one birthday party per year. She was a very organized lady!

tear, but it stung me to be excluded. I doubt if those girls would have made that mistake if their parents had taught them to be mindful of the feelings of others.

Childhood has inevitable bumps in the road, but many of these can be circumstantial. A kid is only a kid for a short period of time. That's why events such as birthday parties are so important. The years will quickly pass, and life's challenges and responsibilities will take hold. Someday your son or daughter will look back, perhaps in the midst of a busy day, and reflect on a significant moment from childhood. Maybe they'll remember a favorite birthday that was celebrated with family and friends or a cherished gift that was received. He or she will recall that memory with warmth and fondness and be grateful to you for making it happen.

Her children arise and call her blessed.
PROVERBS 31:28

CALL OF THE WILD! · *Danae*

FOR A JUNGLE BIRTHDAY EXTRAVAGANZA:

- Send out invitations that include a request to dress in safari-inspired clothing and comfortable shoes.
- Decorate the room with jungle-related stuffed animals, plants, and accessories, which can be purchased at party and toy stores.
- Use plates, napkins, cups, and utensils to fit the theme.
- Have gummy worms on hand. Kids love them!
- Give young guests butterfly nets, squirt guns, and plastic bug collection kits as party favors. (If using Tupperware, remember to poke five holes in each lid.)
- Play jungle tunes, which can be purchased and downloaded online, as background music.

JUNGLE ACTIVITIES:

- Lead the group on a safari to gather exotic specimens with their butterfly nets and collection kits. Safari dads can come in handy here! Bring a whistle to keep the troops in line.
- A piñata is always a hit (literally). Select one to fit the theme, such as a monkey or Toucan bird.
- If your budget allows, rent an inflatable jumping gym. Many come in animal and fantasy shapes. You'll want to send your "jungle critters" home exhausted after a day filled with fun!

Menu

Rainforest Veggies and Dip
Tiger Tails
Cheetah Chips (cheese puffs)
Mini Monkey Dogs with Dipping Sauce
Chocolate Critter Cookies
Rainbow Cupcakes
Jungle Party Punch

TIGER TAILS

1 (14-ounce) bag orange candy
    melting wafers like Wilton's
    Orange Candy Melts
½ cup all-vegetable shortening, divided
½ (14-ounce) bag chocolate candy
    melting wafers
1 (10-ounce) bag pretzel rods

In a large microwave-safe bowl, combine orange candy melting wafers and ¼ cup shortening. Microwave on high for 30 seconds. Stir well. Continue heating for 30 seconds at a time and stirring until melted (approximately 1½ minutes total). In a separate microwave-safe bowl, combine chocolate candy melting wafers and remaining ¼ cup shortening. Microwave on high in 30 second intervals, stirring between each, until melted (approximately 1½ minutes total). Dip each pretzel rod into orange mixture to coat and place on a sheet of parchment paper to dry. Drizzle with melted chocolate in a zigzag fashion to resemble tiger stripes. Store in an airtight container until ready to serve.
Yield: 24 rods

MINI MONKEY DOGS WITH DIPPING SAUCE

1 cup all-purpose flour
⅔ cup yellow cornmeal
2 tablespoons sugar
2 tablespoons dry mustard
1 tablespoon baking powder
¼ teaspoon salt
1 large egg
2 tablespoons vegetable oil
1 cup milk
1 (16-ounce) package smoked
    cocktail wieners
Vegetable oil for frying
Frill toothpicks

Honey-Roasted Barbecue Sauce

¾ cup mayonnaise

¼ cup yellow mustard

¼ cup barbecue sauce

¼ cup honey

To make the barbecue sauce, whisk all ingredients together and set aside.

Line a baking sheet with parchment paper and set aside. To make the mini monkey dogs, combine flour, cornmeal, sugar, dry mustard, baking powder, and salt in a medium bowl. Add egg, oil, and milk. Whisk to combine. Roll wieners in batter to coat. Place on the baking sheet and then put it in the freezer for 30 minutes. Roll wieners in batter a second time to fully coat. Return wieners to freezer to keep cold while oil is heating. Fill a deep pan ⅔ full with vegetable oil. Heat oil to 350°. Fry corn dogs in batches of 4 for 3 to 5 minutes or until golden brown. Drain on paper towels. Stick frill toothpicks into wieners and serve immediately with honey-roasted barbecue sauce. (If young children will be eating corn dogs, snip off the sharp ends of the toothpicks.)
Yield: Approximately 24 corn dogs

Rainbow Cupcakes

1 box white cake mix

1 bottle colored sprinkles

Orange Icing

1 (8-ounce) package cream cheese, softened

5 cups powdered sugar

1 tablespoon fresh orange zest

2 tablespoons orange juice

2 teaspoons vanilla extract

1 teaspoon orange extract

Prepare cake mix as directed, but add a portion of the colored sprinkles to the batter. Beat for an additional 30 seconds. Fill prepared muffin cups ⅔ full. Bake as directed on the box or until a wooden pick inserted into the center comes out clean. Remove from oven and cool completely.

To make orange icing, in a medium bowl beat cream cheese at high speed with an electric mixer until smooth. Add powdered sugar, zest, juice, and extracts, mixing until combined. Place orange frosting in a pastry bag fitted with a star tip. Pipe icing onto cupcakes. Garnish with colored sprinkles.
Yield: 24 cupcakes

CHOCOLATE CRITTER COOKIES

1 cup unsalted butter, softened
½ cup powdered sugar
2 (1-ounce) squares semisweet baking
    chocolate, melted and cooled
½ teaspoon vanilla extract
2 cups all-purpose flour
½ teaspoon baking powder
¼ teaspoon salt

MERINGUE POWDER ICING

¼ cup cold water
3 tablespoons meringue powder
2 cups powdered sugar, sifted
Assorted gel paste food colorings
Assorted colored sprinkles and
    sanding sugars

In a large bowl, beat butter and powdered sugar together with an electric mixer at medium speed until creamy. Stir in the melted chocolate and vanilla. In a medium bowl, sift together flour, baking powder, and salt. Gradually add flour mixture to the chocolate mixture, beating to combine. Shape into a disk and wrap with plastic wrap. Refrigerate for at least 1 hour. Preheat oven to 350°. Line 2 cookie sheets with parchment paper and set aside. On a lightly floured surface, roll dough to ¼-inch thickness. Using 2½- to 3-inch animal cookie cutters, cut out as many cookies as possible, rerolling scraps only twice. Place cookies on prepared baking sheets. Bake for 12 minutes per batch. Cool on pans for 5 minutes. Remove to wire racks to cool completely.

To make the meringue powder icing, whisk together water and meringue powder in a small bowl until frothy. Add powdered sugar, whisking until smooth. Divide mixture into several bowls. Whisk in gel paste food colors to achieve desired color. Immediately apply icing to cookies using small pastry brushes. Before icing dries, decorate with sanding sugars and sprinkles. Set on parchment paper to dry. Store cookies in an airtight container at room temperature.
Yield: 24 cookies

JUNGLE PARTY PUNCH

2 cups water
1 cup sugar
1 (3-ounce) package lime flavored
    gelatin
2 cups cold pineapple juice
1 (2-liter) bottle cold lemon-lime
    carbonated beverage
1 quart lemon sherbet, slightly
    softened

In a small saucepan, bring water and sugar to a boil over high heat. Cook for approximately 5 minutes or until sugar is dissolved. Remove from heat and whisk in gelatin. Stir for 2 minutes or until completely dissolved. Add pineapple juice. Cool to room temperature. Just before serving, pour mixture into punch bowl or other serving container. Add carbonated beverage and sherbet.
Yield: 1 gallon

FOURTH OF JULY

HOST A STAR-SPANGLED BARBECUE TO
PAY TRIBUTE TO OUR GREAT COUNTRY
AND THANK GOD FOR OUR FREEDOM.

INDEPENDENCE DAY ,
Shirley

Fourth of July celebration with friends

Many Americans, especially members of the younger generation, have little or no knowledge of our nation's history. How many high school and college students have any understanding of the American Revolution or the terrible wars that followed? Do they know that the first Independence Day occurred in Philadelphia in 1776 or why it was so significant?

The Declaration of Independence, the document we celebrate on the Fourth of July, cost the lives of many good men. Some of them were only teenagers. When Patrick Henry said, "Give me liberty or give me death," he was not just uttering a phrase but expressing his deep conviction and willingness to die for what he believed. Yet without the sacrifices of those who fought for our freedom, we might be living in tyranny today.

The Fourth of July, then, is more than just a national holiday to enjoy backyard barbecues, baseball games, and displays of colorful fireworks. May I suggest that you save a few minutes later that evening for your family and friends to read and reflect on the Declaration of Independence or the Bill of Rights? One of your children might want to prepare for and recite the Preamble to the Constitution. It reads:

> " We the people of the United States, in order to form a more perfect
> union, establish justice, insure domestic tranquility, provide for the
> common defense, promote the general welfare, and secure the
> blessings of liberty to ourselves and our posterity, do ordain and
> establish this Constitution for the United States of America. "

We owe it to our great nation and its forefathers to become familiar with our past, because if we don't know where we have been, we won't know who we are or where we are headed.

Before the barbeque gets underway, instead of just thanking God for the food, you may also wish to thank Him for our freedom. Another good idea is to have everyone sing "God Bless America." The Fourth of July is the perfect occasion to be reminded of how precious the gift of freedom is.

Menu

All-American Burgers with Special Sauce
Condiments
Bacon and Herb Potato Salad
Grandma Alma's Baked Beans
Corn on the Cob • Veggies and Dip
Watermelon Slices • Chips
Red, White, and Blue Trifle
Cola Chocolate Sheet Cake
Sparkling Cranberry Punch

ALL-AMERICAN BURGERS WITH SPECIAL SAUCE

2 pounds ground chuck
2 teaspoons Dijon-style mustard
¼ teaspoon hot pepper sauce
1 clove garlic, minced
1 teaspoon salt
½ teaspoon ground black pepper

SPECIAL SAUCE

½ cup light mayonnaise-style salad dressing
¼ cup creamy French dressing
¼ cup pickle relish
1 teaspoon sugar
⅓ teaspoon ground black pepper

Preheat grill to medium-high (350° to 400°). In a large bowl, mix ground chuck with mustard, hot pepper sauce, garlic, salt, and black pepper. Shape into 10 patties. Grill patties until desired level of doneness (4 to 6 minutes per side). Serve on warm, buttered hamburger buns with special sauce. Garnish with shredded lettuce, sliced tomato, and sliced red onion.
Yield: 10 burgers

To make the special sauce, mix salad dressings, pickle relish, sugar, and black pepper in a small bowl. Refrigerate until needed.
Yield: approximately 1 cup

Every good and perfect gift is from above, coming down from the Father of the heavenly lights.
JAMES 1:17

Bacon and Herb Potato Salad

1 (3-pound) bag small red potatoes,
    quartered
8 sprigs fresh thyme
2 tablespoons vegetable oil
1 teaspoon salt
1 teaspoon ground black pepper
¾ cup mayonnaise
¼ cup fresh lemon juice
8 slices of bacon, cooked and crumbled
½ cup chopped green onion

*Preheat oven to 400°. Spray a baking sheet
with no-stick cooking spray and set aside. In a
large bowl, combine potatoes, thyme, oil, salt,
and pepper. Mix well to coat. Arrange potatoes
in a single layer on the prepared baking sheet.
Bake until potatoes are brown and tender,
approximately 30 minutes. Allow to cool on
a wire rack for 20 minutes. In a large bowl,
combine mayonnaise and lemon juice. Add
potatoes, bacon, and onion, tossing to coat.
Cover and refrigerate for at least 30 minutes.
Yield: 6 to 8 servings*

Grandma Alma's Baked Beans

1 large can (1 pound, 15 ounces)
    baked beans
1 cup dark corn syrup
½ cup brown sugar
½ cup ketchup
1 yellow onion, grated

*Combine all ingredients in a bean pot or a 9 x
13-inch pan. Bake at 350° for 45 minutes or
until juice begins to thicken.
Yield: 12 servings*

49

RED, WHITE, AND BLUE TRIFLE

1 (16-ounce) container frozen
    nondairy whipped topping, thawed
1 (8-ounce) package cream cheese,
    softened
1 (7-ounce) jar marshmallow creme
1 tablespoon lemon zest
2 tablespoons fresh lemon juice
½ cup powdered sugar
2 cans cherry pie filling (gel, not juice)
4 cups fresh blueberries
1 prepared angel food cake, cut into
    1-inch cubes
Nondairy whipped topping, cherry
    filling, and fresh blueberries
    mixture for garnish

*In a large bowl, combine whipped topping
(reserving a small portion for garnish),
cream cheese, marshmallow creme, lemon
zest, and lemon juice. Beat at medium
speed with an electric mixer until smooth.
Gradually add powdered sugar, beating
until combined. Set aside. In a medium
bowl, pour in the cherry pie filling, sweeten
to taste with powdered sugar, and fold
in the blueberries. Set mixture aside
(including a small portion for garnish). To
assemble the trifle, layer half of the cream
mixture in the bottom of the trifle bowl.
Top cream mixture with half the cake cubes.
Top cake cubes with half of the cherry and
blueberry mixture. Repeat layers. Garnish
with reserved nondairy whipped topping,
and reserved cherry and blueberry mixture.
Yield: 12 servings*

Cola Chocolate Sheet Cake

4 cups all-purpose flour
8 tablespoons unsweetened cocoa
    powder
3 teaspoons cinnamon
1 teaspoon salt
2 teaspoons baking soda
4 cups sugar
1 pound butter (4 sticks)
4 eggs
1 cup buttermilk
4 teaspoons vanilla
2 cups cola beverage

Icing

½ cup butter
½ cup plus 1 tablespoon cola
    beverage
6 tablespoons unsweetened cocoa
    powder
1 cup chopped pecans
2 teaspoons vanilla extract
2 (1-pound) boxes powdered sugar

Grease and flour an 11 x 17–inch pan. Sift together the dry ingredients and set aside. In a saucepan, heat the butter and cola until the butter melts. Add the eggs, vanilla, and buttermilk and mix well. Add the liquid to the dry ingredients and beat until smooth (batter will be thin). Pour into the prepared pan and bake at 350° for 30 minutes.

To make the icing, heat the butter and cola in a saucepan. Do not boil. Add the cocoa, vanilla, and powdered sugar. Mix well. Pour over the warm cake (the cake must be iced while warm). Sprinkle with chopped pecans. Yield: 16 servings

Sparkling Cranberry Punch

1 (12-ounce) can frozen lemonade
    concentrate, thawed
1½ cups cold water
1 (64-ounce) bottle cranberry juice
    cocktail, chilled
4 (12-ounce) cans ginger ale, chilled

Mix the lemonade concentrate and cold water in a pitcher. Pour into a punch bowl or large bowl and add the cranberry juice cocktail. Just before serving, add the ginger ale and ice cubes. Serve in a punch bowl, a serving container, or in individual glasses. Yield: 24 servings (¾ cup each)

51

BEACH OR LAKE COOKOUT

BEFORE THE WARM WEATHER DISAPPEARS, PREPARE
SOME DELICIOUS RECIPES, GRAB YOUR FRIENDS,
AND HEAD FOR A SCENIC SPOT ON THE WATER.

Summer's Last Big Hurrah · *Danae*

For eleven years I've hosted an annual "end of summer beach barbecue" in September. You might think the weather would be too chilly at that time of year for such an event, but in Southern California where I reside, the temperatures are still warm.

Friends who attend this barbecue come from all walks of life—singles, marrieds, parents, children, and even grandparents. They trudge through the sand carrying towels and lawn chairs, ready to roast wieners, play games, and enjoy Christian fellowship.

As the hostess I make it a point to arrive early so I can set up two folding tables with assorted drinks, hotdog condiments, and homemade desserts. It isn't long before friends crowd the tables with items they've signed up to bring, such as napkins, plastic utensils, veggies and dip, chips and salsa, cookies, and other finger foods.

After doing a little munching, some people jump into the ocean while others engage in games, such as the water balloon toss. At approximately five o'clock, one of the guys leads the group in prayer, and we thank God for our food. Then it's weenie roastin' time! Some folks use sophisticated grills while others cook their links retro style on straightened wire coat hangers. S'mores are part of the fun too, resulting in sticky fingers and blackened teeth.

When the sun goes down, a pastor friend leads us in a bonfire devotional. It's a picturesque setting as people sit around the fire pit on lawn chairs and beach towels, listening to the pastor share while logs glow and crackle.

My idea for this event was born out of my days in my church's high school group. Our youth pastor held beach barbecues during the summer months where we all roasted hotdogs on wire hangers, sat around the bonfire, and listened to him teach us about Jesus. I enjoyed these times of fellowship so much that years later I began hosting my own beach barbecues. The first event saw fifteen attendees, but as friends began to invite friends, the numbers grew. Now we average forty. It's exciting to see how the Lord has blessed these get-togethers through the years.

I believe the main reason for His blessing is because we honor Him. Sure, I could invite friends to the beach for no purpose other than to enjoy the sun, fun, and good food, but how much more significant our time together becomes when we focus on the One who created that beautiful place.

This is true for any social gathering among believers. The Lord takes pleasure in seeing His followers enjoying one another and having fun, but He wants us to acknowledge Him and allow Him to be at the center of our activities. By doing so, our events take on greater meaning, and friends part ways feeling closer to each other and more refreshed than when they arrived.

A beach or lake cookout is a great way to round up friends for some fun. I've been amazed at the response my annual beach barbecue has generated. I guess there's truth to the saying "If you invite them, they will come." People are often just waiting for someone to take the initiative.

So whether you eat or drink or whatever you do, do it all for the glory of God. 1 Corinthians 10:31

Hotdogs (regular and turkey)
Condiments
Chips and Salsa
Veggie Platter with Dip
Orange Fruit Dip with Assorted Fruit
S'mores
Fresh Peach Cobbler
Carrot Ginger Sheet Cake
Assorted Beverages and Bottled Water

ORANGE FRUIT DIP WITH ASSORTED FRUITS

1 (8-ounce) package cream cheese, softened
1 (7-ounce) jar marshmallow creme
1 (16-ounce) container frozen nondairy whipped topping, thawed
2 tablespoons honey
1 tablespoon fresh orange zest
1 teaspoon vanilla extract
¼ teaspoon ground cinnamon
Assorted fresh fruits

In a medium bowl, beat cream cheese at medium-high speed with an electric mixer until smooth. Add marshmallow creme and continue beating until combined. Add whipped topping, honey, orange zest, vanilla, and cinnamon, beating until smooth. Refrigerate for at least 2 hours before serving. While in transit, keep dip on ice in a cooler. Serve with assorted fruit, which has been cut into large pieces and skewered with frill toothpicks.
Yield: 10 servings

Fresh Peach Cobbler

½ cup butter or margarine, melted
2 cups granulated sugar, divided
1 cup all-purpose flour
1 teaspoon baking powder
Dash of salt
¾ cup low-fat milk
6 fresh peaches, peeled and sliced or
    1 (29-ounce) can of sliced
    peaches (with juice)
Vanilla ice cream (optional)

Preheat oven to 350°. Pour melted butter into a 9 x 9-inch baking dish. In a large bowl, combine 1½ cups sugar, flour, baking powder, salt, and milk. Pour mixture over the melted butter. Pour peaches and their juice over the flour mixture. Do not stir. Bake for 40 minutes or until golden brown. When cobbler looks bubbly, pour ½ cup sugar on top and gently press into the fruit with the back of a small spoon. Put back into the oven for 2 or 3 minutes. Serve with vanilla ice cream (optional).
Yield: 8 servings

CARROT GINGER SHEET CAKE

2 cups all-purpose flour
2 cups granulated sugar
2 teaspoons baking powder
½ teaspoon baking soda
4 eggs
3 cups finely shredded carrots
¾ cup cooking oil
¾ cup mixed dried fruit bits
2 teaspoons grated fresh ginger
    (or ¾ teaspoon ground ginger)
1 cup finely chopped pecans, toasted

ORANGE CREAM CHEESE ICING

2 (3-ounce) packages cream cheese,
    softened
½ cup butter, softened
1 tablespoon orange juice
4¾ cups powdered sugar, sifted
½ teaspoon finely shredded
    orange peel

Preheat oven to 350°. Grease and flour a 9 x 13-inch glass baking dish. Set aside. In a large bowl, stir together flour, sugar, baking powder, and baking soda. Set aside. In a medium bowl, beat eggs and stir in shredded carrot, oil, dried fruit bits, and ginger. Stir egg mixture into the flour mixture. Pour batter into prepared pan. Bake 30 to 35 minutes or until a wooden toothpick inserted into the center comes out clean. Cool before frosting.

To make orange cream cheese icing, combine the cream cheese, butter, and orange juice in a large bowl. Beat with an electric mixer on medium speed until smooth. Gradually add 2 cups of the sifted powdered sugar, beating until mixed. Gradually add an additional 2½ to 2¾ cups sifted powdered sugar to make a spreading consistency. Stir in ½ teaspoon finely shredded orange peel. Frost cake after it has cooled and sprinkle with toasted chopped pecans.
Yield: 16 servings

56

AUTUMN HARVEST TEA

MY FRIEND JENNY · *Shirley*

hen we moved to Colorado in 1991, I wanted to get acquainted with our new neighbors as soon as possible. It didn't take me long to get started. As I was pulling into our driveway on the day of our arrival, I saw an elderly lady sitting in her front yard next door. She was wearing a large hat and working on an oil landscape that sat on an easel. When she saw me, she stood up and walked over to my car window. I introduced myself to my new neighbor, and she said her name was Jenny. It was the beginning of a very sweet friendship.

Jenny was a spunky lady in her mid-eighties. Within minutes she leaned into my car window and said, "You don't have a dog, do you?" She told me she didn't like barkers and that dogs in our area had to be kept on a leash. I told Jenny we had a wonderful dog named Mitzi that almost never barked and that she was a house dog. Danae and her dad had rescued this lonely mutt from the pound, and she had turned out to be the most loving, beautiful, and gentle dog we had ever owned. Jenny never had reason to be irritated by Mitzi, but she had wanted to get some things straight right from the beginning. There was something charming about her brisk and direct manner.

The more I got to know Jenny, the more I admired her. I learned she had been married three times and had walked through tragic illnesses with each husband. They had all passed on. Jenny lived alone, but she was determined to enjoy her remaining years to their fullest. She was very resourceful. Not only did she paint with oils, but she continued to travel abroad with family and friends. She loved people and was very social. She urged me often not to let the busyness of life keep me from sitting, talking, and listening to people. I knew she was speaking of herself and her desire for fellowship.

The years passed quickly, and Jenny began to show signs of physical deterioration, especially her night vision. However, she was not about to surrender her independence. She still drove her car after dark, and I worried about her safety. She attached a tennis ball to her antennae so she could find her car in parking lots. One night my husband and I were driving home when we realized that Jenny was driving in front of us. She was going very slow and weaving from side to side. When we came to a bend in the road, Jenny brought her car to a complete stop as she tried to figure out where she was. Finally she crept around the curve and made her way home. I don't think she ever knew we were behind her. What an indomitable spirit this precious lady had.

I began to be very concerned about Jenny, not only physically but spiritually. She would soon leave this earth, and I didn't know if she knew Jesus Christ as her personal Lord and Savior. I felt responsible to make sure that she heard the good news of eternal life. Jenny never mentioned the subject, which made it difficult. Finally I decided to invite her to my house for tea and let the Lord lead our conversation. I prayed that I would have an opportunity to share my faith with her. I set out my fine china and placed some cakes on a glass plate. We had a lovely time sipping our tea and chitchatting. As we were ending our time together, the Lord gave me an opportunity to share my faith with this special lady. Jenny assured me that she was ready to meet the Lord and even invited me to attend her church with her. I felt a peace when she left and was glad I had followed the Lord's leading.

Jenny has now passed on to her heavenly home, and another couple has moved into her house. Life goes on. Looking back I wish I had spent more time with my elderly friend just sitting, talking, and listening. She was right. I often let the busyness of life rob me of those special times when I could have had tea with Jenny and gleaned from her wisdom and experience. I wish I could talk to her again, just friend to friend. She might even have taught me to paint.

If I become a widow someday, which happens to the vast majority of married women, I hope I will retain the same zest for life that Jenny enjoyed. Her circumstances had been difficult, having said goodbye to three loving husbands. Nevertheless, she took life as it came. I also hope when and if I am alone and aging, a loving neighbor will reach out to me in friendship as I tried to do for Jenny.

I have a dear friend who has a ministry to elderly people who are in nursing homes. She said that eighty percent of them *never* have one visitor. No one is there to ask about their childhood years, the people they loved, or the babies they bore and reared. They sit day after day with their memories. It breaks my heart to see how these special people are neglected.

Another friend told me he misdialed a telephone number one day, and an older woman answered. Realizing he had made a mistake, this friend started to apologize. The woman on the other end of the line said, "Oh, please don't hang up. I am eighty-two years old, and no one ever calls me. Would you talk to me?"

I pray that the Lord will help me remember that hospitality should include not just our established friends and colleagues, but also the lonely person next door who is desperate for an expression of human kindness. Jenny taught me that.

Whether you have a tea party for two or several, may the love of Christ flow through you to bless those in need of friendship.

Truly I tell you, whatever you did for one of the least of these brothers and sisters of mine, you did for me. Matthew 25:40

Pumpkin Bread and Cream Cheese Sandwiches
Deviled Egg Sandwiches (brown bread)
Orange Cream Cheese and Olive Sandwiches (white bread)
Fresh Fruit Salad in Autumn Colors
Pumpkin Trifle • Mixed Nuts
Orange Spice Black Tea • Darjeeling Decaffeinated Tea

PUMPKIN BREAD AND CREAM CHEESE SANDWICHES

1 (15-ounce) can pumpkin

3 eggs

¾ cup oil

1 teaspoon vanilla

2 teaspoons cinnamon

1½ teaspoons ginger

½ teaspoon ground cloves

1½ teaspoons sugar

1½ teaspoons baking soda

½ teaspoon salt

2½ cups flour

1 (8-ounce) package cream cheese, softened

1 (3.4-ounce) package instant vanilla pudding, prepared

1 (3.4-ounce) package instant butterscotch pudding, prepared

1 (16-ounce) container frozen nondairy whipped topping, thawed and divided

1 small bag chopped walnuts

In a mixing bowl, combine pumpkin, eggs, oil, and vanilla. Beat for 2 minutes. With exception to the cream cheese, add the rest of the ingredients. Beat for an additional 2 minutes. Grease a 9 x 4-inch bread pan. Pour mixture into pan and bake at 350° for 45 to 50 minutes. After bread has cooled, slice into small squares and spread with cream cheese to make tea sandwiches.
Yield: 24 sandwiches

PUMPKIN TRIFLE

1 spice cake mix, prepared

1 (15-ounce) can pumpkin

½ teaspoon cinnamon

⅛ teaspoon nutmeg

1¼ cup cold milk

Crumble spice cake and divide in half. Set aside. In a small bowl, combine pumpkin, cinnamon, nutmeg, and milk. Mix well by hand. Divide in half. Set aside. To assemble the trifle, layer half the crumbled spice cake in the bottom of the trifle bowl. Top cake layer with half of the pumpkin mixture. Top pumpkin mixture with half of the nondairy whipped topping. Top nondairy whipped topping with butterscotch pudding. Top butterscotch pudding with other half of crumbled spice cake. Top spice cake with other half of pumpkin. Top pumpkin with vanilla pudding. Top vanilla pudding with other half of nondairy whipped topping. Sprinkle walnuts on top. Store in the refrigerator until ready to serve.
Yield: 10 to 12 servings

BACK TO SCHOOL

WHO KNEW GOING BACK TO SCHOOL COULD
NOT ONLY BE FUN BUT TASTY TOO? NOTHING
SPELLS COMFORT LIKE A SAVORY BOWL OF
CHILI PAIRED WITH WARM CORNBREAD.

A New Chapter · *Danae*

It's not surprising to hear moms cheering and kids jeering as the long days of summer come to an end. Supply stores start seeing rulers, pencils, and folders fly off the shelves as students prepare to head back to school.

In my own childhood experience, the weeks that preceded the start of a new school year were filled with great anticipation. I hoped I would be assigned to the cool teacher's classroom, and I wanted my best girlfriend to be there too. My parents had an entirely different way of thinking. They prayed that the Lord would place me where He wanted me. Knowing they had prayed this way helped me to understand that the classroom I got assigned to was where I was supposed to be.

Before the first day of school, my mom and I would go clothes shopping. We would find cute dresses at my favorite boutique called The Adorable Shop. At the end of the day, we would stumble through the front door, packages in hand, and head for my bedroom to unload. No matter how tired I felt, I was eager to model my new clothes for Daddy. I would try on each garment, and then he and my mom would decide what was worth keeping and what should be returned. I used to love it when my dad would take one look at my outfit and say, "Now that's sharp!" I knew I had picked a winner.

Despite the warm California weather in September, I preferred wearing my new clothes right away. I'd trot off to school in a cowl-necked sweater and jumper dress, but by the afternoon I'd be stretching the neck of that sweater to get some air. When a fellow classmate inevitably asked, "Aren't you hot?" I'd smile and say, "Not really." As far as I was concerned, a bit of discomfort was a small price to pay for the privilege of wearing something new.

I look back on those days with amusement. It's clear to me now that my desire to wear new clothes was associated, at least in part, with the uneasiness I felt about starting a new year of school.

It's common for children to experience back-to-school jitters. They wonder if they'll like their teachers, who will be in their classes, and how difficult their exams will be. Parents can become anxious too.

One way you can ease the tension is by creating a little fun. On the first day of school, why not prepare something warm and "kid approved" for dinner, such as chili and cornbread, and bake a favorite dessert? During the meal encourage conversation by asking questions regarding your child's first impressions of his or her teacher and classmates. Listen carefully and offer suggestions. You might want to finish off your time together by playing a game or taking the dog for a walk—something carefree to take the edge off the day.

Another idea is to host a Saturday get-acquainted lunch for your son or daughter's classmates at the start of the school year. Invite their teacher too! You can keep it simple by whipping up a few finger foods and having some games ready. A casual get-together is a good way to help everyone feel more at ease as they coast into a new school year.

Finally let me encourage you to insert love notes in your child's lunch box. My mother used to do that from time to time, and it meant so much to me. When I would open my lunch pail and find a little message from her, assuring me that she was thinking about me and loving me, it brought joy and comfort to my day. I saved many of her notes and still have some of them today.

The love and support of a dedicated parent makes every kid's school experience a little easier.

Parents are the pride of their children.
PROVERBS 17:6

Ground Turkey Chili
Eva Lena's Southern Cornbread
Peanut Butter Cookies
Milk

GROUND TURKEY CHILI

1 pound ground turkey
1 (15-ounce) can chili beans
    (with liquid)
1 (15-ounce) can kidney beans
    (with liquid)
1 (1.25- to 1.48-ounce) packet chili
    seasoning mix
1½ cups water
Shredded cheese for garnish

In a large skillet, fry ground turkey until crumbly. Add cans of beans. Add seasoning mix. Add water to desired consistency. Heat until boiling, then reduce heat, cover, and simmer for 20 minutes. Garnish with shredded cheese.
Yield: 6 servings

EVA LENA'S SOUTHERN CORNBREAD

2 eggs
½ cup oil
1 cup milk
1 (14.75-ounce) can cream style corn
1 white onion, chopped
1 cup cornmeal (yellow or white)
1 teaspoon salt
1 teaspoon baking soda
1 pound cheddar cheese, shredded

Mix eggs, oil, milk, and corn. Add onions and cheese. Stir. Sift dry ingredients. Add to mixture and let set for a few minutes. Grease and heat large skillet in a 400° oven. Pour mixture into hot skillet and bake approximately 30 minutes or until golden brown.
Yield: 10 servings

BIBLE STUDY

As you and your friends get comfy for an in-depth study of God's Word, pour steaming cups of cider and serve it with a scrumptious dessert.

LIGHT THE WAY · *Danae*

My mother has always had a love for the Word of God. As a young girl, she attended a summer children's Bible study that was led by a woman in her neighborhood. She initially was more enthused about the lemonade and cookies, but soon became captivated by the Bible stories, which were illustrated on flannel boards. That experience made such a strong impression on my mom that she decided to host her own children's study after she was grown.

She began by printing flyers and asking Ryan and me to distribute one to every home in our neighborhood. (We were still kids at the time.) The flyers informed parents of my mom's plan to start a weekly summer study that focused on Bible stories and not theology.

Approximately fifteen children showed up at our home the first day. As the weeks progressed, they began to invite friends, and soon our family room was brimming with boys and girls. My mom kept the Kool-Aid flowing and served homemade cookies. Then following the example of the woman in her neighborhood from many years earlier, she used a flannel board to teach Bible stories. They included Shadrach, Meshach, and Abednego, Daniel in the lions' den, and David and Goliath.

The children were asked to memorize one Bible verse each week. If they accomplished that goal, they received the reward of reaching into a grab bag and pulling out a treat. The bag was full of inexpensive toys and lollipops. My mom also had a fishbowl filled with pennies that was used for the same purpose. The children would reach into the bowl and grasp as many pennies as they could hold. Of course a fistful of pennies amounts to less than one dollar, but the kids thought they had hit the jackpot.

BIBLE STUDY TIP: When Jesus taught the people, He fed them. As a child, I used to watch my mom preparing hot beverages and coffee cake, which I always sampled, for her morning study group. There's something uniquely satisfying about combining food with the Bible learning experience. Our minds and spirits become strengthened and refreshed by His powerful Word and the provision He has set before us.

On the last day of the classes, my mom gave them an opportunity to receive Jesus as their Savior. One of the children who accepted the invitation was a girl who lived next door. She bowed her head and prayed while my mother recited the sinner's prayer. Years later my mom ran in to her at the supermarket, and by that time this young lady was married with kids of her own. During their conversation she recalled the neighborhood Bible study with fondness and talked about how much it had impacted her. She said that she was continuing to live for Christ and had been taking her children to church, all because of that decision she made in our family room at twelve years of age.

My mom's sphere of influence extended beyond children. One day a Christian friend stopped by our house to discuss her burden for unsaved women in the neighborhood. She asked my mom if she would be willing to join her in starting a weekly morning Bible study. My mom agreed, and the two women set about getting the word out.

When the study first began, some of the ladies who attended didn't even know what the book of Genesis was about! They quickly grew in their knowledge, and eventually each of the unsaved women gave her heart to the Lord, including the mayor's wife! It was a feeling of great accomplishment for my mom and her friend, who had been praying diligently for those who were lost.

Through the years my mother has participated in other forms of outreach, including being a discussion leader for Bible Study Fellowship and hosting an evening series led by a Bible teacher. With each endeavor she's been mindful not to exceed her limitations. She's made a point to commit to a certain period of time, knowing that when she had met her obligation, she would seek God's direction on whether or not to continue. I think that's a good formula for all women in ministry to embrace, especially those with young children.

My mom has instilled in me the importance of studying and memorizing Scripture, and her example is one of the reasons why I've hosted a Friday night Bible study in my home for seven years. I view the Bible as the greatest resource for every area of our lives. It provides insight, direction, and God's eternal promises. Everything else in this world will pass away, but the Word of God will stand firm throughout eternity.

The grass withers and the flowers fall, but the word of our God endures forever. Isaiah 40:8

Apple Nut Cake with Lemon Cheese Icing
Veggies and Dip
Fruit Plate
Caramel Corn
Mixed Peanuts and Candy Corn
Hot Apple Cider

APPLE NUT CAKE WITH LEMON CHEESE ICING

2 eggs, beaten
2 cups sugar
1 teaspoon vanilla
½ cup oil
2 cups all-purpose flour
2 teaspoons baking soda
2 teaspoons cinnamon
¾ teaspoon salt
1 cup chopped walnuts
6 pippin apples, finely shredded

LEMON CHEESE ICING

1 (3-ounce) package cream cheese,
   at room temperature
2 tablespoons milk
½ cup butter or margarine, softened
1½ cups powdered sugar
1 teaspoon lemon juice
1 teaspoon vanilla
Dash of salt
½ cup chopped walnuts

In a medium bowl, combine eggs, sugar, and vanilla. Beat with an electric mixer until blended. Add oil and continue beating until smooth. Add flour, baking soda, cinnamon, and salt. Stir all ingredients by hand until well blended. Add walnuts and apples. Stir thoroughly. Pour into floured and greased 11 x 7-inch pan. Bake at 325° for 1 hour or until golden brown.

To make icing, combine cream cheese, milk, butter or margarine, powdered sugar, lemon juice, vanilla, and salt in a medium bowl. Beat with an electric mixer at medium speed until fluffy. Stir in walnuts. Frost cake when cool.
Yield: 15 servings

Hot Apple Cider

> 2 quarts apple cider
> ²/₃ cup golden brown sugar
> ¼ teaspoon salt
> 6 whole cloves
> 6 whole allspice
> 4 sticks cinnamon

Combine all ingredients in pan on low heat. Bring to a boil. Simmer for 5 minutes. Remove from heat. Strain. Put spices in a tea ball and put back into cider (optional). Serve cider hot. Suggestion: Add a touch of color by placing half of an orange slice and a stick of cinnamon in each cup.
Yield: 10 to 12 servings

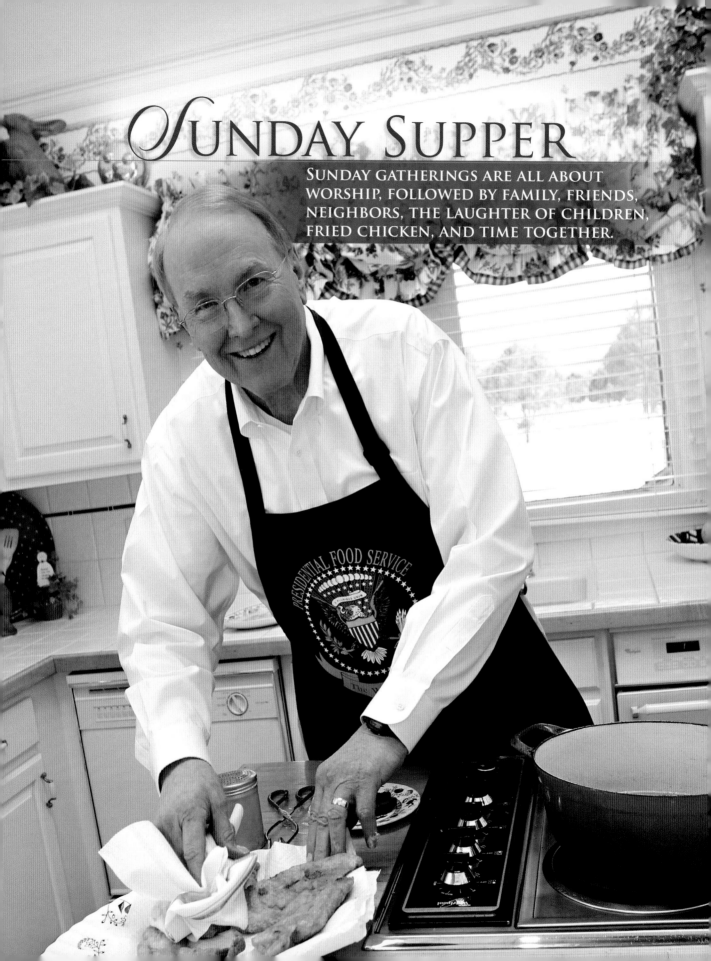

SUNDAY SUPPER

SUNDAY GATHERINGS ARE ALL ABOUT
WORSHIP, FOLLOWED BY FAMILY, FRIENDS,
NEIGHBORS, THE LAUGHTER OF CHILDREN,
FRIED CHICKEN, AND TIME TOGETHER.

COMPANY'S COMIN' · *Danae*

Among my many fond memories of childhood were the Sunday afternoons spent with friends. I can recall running to my mother when church ended and asking if so-and-so could come to our house for lunch and playtime. My mom usually agreed, although she insisted that I couldn't ask her this question in the presence of whomever I was inviting, to avoid an awkward situation. Upon receiving permission I would hurry back to my friend to exclaim that my mom had given the okay.

We would then climb into the car with my family and go to lunch—either to our home where my parents prepared the meal or to a restaurant. I was always proud to bring a friend around my parents because I knew she would be treated kindly, regardless of her tender age. My mom and dad made a point of asking questions and showing genuine interest. My dad even mentioned her name in his prayer before the meal, thanking God for her friendship with me and for making it possible to spend time together. My girlfriend and I usually spent the rest of the afternoon playing with Barbie dolls or engaging in a backyard activity while my parents took their Sunday afternoon naps. Then it was off to church again for the evening service. What fun days those were!

One Sunday afternoon my mom received a phone call from the social secretary for the class my dad taught. The woman told my mom, "A young couple, who apparently lives nearby, visited our church today. No one knows them personally, but we would like to make them feel welcome. We need someone to invite them over tonight for a meal and a 'get acquainted' time after the evening service. Would you and Jim want to reach out to them in this way?"

My mom first thought it would be inconvenient. Instead of napping they would have to straighten the house and go to the store to buy food. Then the meal had to be cooked, and other preparations would have to be made for their guests. Nevertheless my mom agreed to call the couple and invite them to our house after the service. They accepted and soon knocked on the front door. It turned out to be a very pleasant evening, and lifelong friendships resulted. After the meal my dad discovered that his guest, Doc Heatherly, had heard him speak on the subject of discipline recently and was very impressed. My dad told him that he had been thinking about writing a book about raising children. What he didn't know was that Doc had been a vice president of Word Publishers (a Christian-based company) and that he could help my dad find a publisher.

The next day while at the medical school where he was a professor, my father received phone calls from two of the publishers Doc had called. Both of them offered contracts for a book, and six months later *Dare to Discipline* was written and published. It is still in the bookstores forty-two years later and has sold more than four million copies! That was the beginning of my dad's writing career. Thirty-four more books followed. It all started with an act of kindness to a young man and woman who were visiting their church.

Romans 12:13 instructs us to, "share with the Lord's people who are in need. Practice hospitality." Clearly God wants to exhibit His love to those whom He brings into our lives. What better way to see Christ's light shining through us than by inviting people into our homes to converse with warmly and share good food? We don't need to prepare a fancy meal and have china and silver on display. In fact the night my parents entertained the publisher and his wife, my mom served a simple taco salad. The important thing is to be available and to use those opportunities to minister to the needs of others.

Hospitality is an essential part of Christian living. Why not invite at least one person to your home this week to share Sunday supper?

And do not forget to do good and to share with others, for with such sacrifices God is pleased. Hebrews 13:16

1. Prepare raw chicken breasts and season one side with salt and pepper.

2. Dredge the seasoned side of chicken in flour, and then season and flour the other side.

3. Test the temperature of the oil by dropping in small pieces of bread.

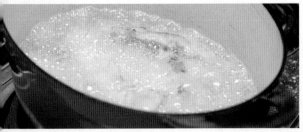

4. Place the chicken in a deep fryer, piece by piece.

DR. DOBSON'S TEXAS FRIED CHICKEN AND CHICKEN GRAVY

(This recipe was given to Dr. Dobson by his mother, one of the best cooks the South ever produced!)

Skinless, bone-in chicken breasts
(as many as you need)
All-purpose flour
Salt and pepper
Canola oil

Wash chicken breasts and remove skin and fatty tissue. Slice each breast into 2 pieces (cut 1 all-meat piece ¼- to ½-inch thick and the other ¼-inch thick meat with bone attached). Place all pieces in bowl of water. Pour enough oil into a large frying pan to cover the bottom approximately 1 inch deep. Heat until oil gently bubbles. The temperature of the oil is the key to the success of this dish! Test the oil by dropping in a small piece of white bread. If the bread floats and quickly turns a golden brown, the oil is ready. While oil is heating, pour enough flour on a large sheet of wax paper to heavily coat the chicken. Place 1 piece of chicken in your palm and salt and pepper it generously. Place the seasoned side of the chicken onto the mound of flour. Coat that side well. Salt and pepper the other side. Dredge the chicken in flour and then set it aside. (Never layer the chicken pieces, even after they're cooked, because the coating will come off). When the oil is ready, place chicken in the pan, piece by piece. Cook 1 side until golden brown, which

75

should take 4 to 5 minutes. Turn to fry the other side. Remove chicken piece by piece. Place them in a large bowl that has been lined with paper towels. Blot excess oil from top of chicken.

Chicken Gravy

6 tablespoons pan drippings
6 tablespoons all-purpose flour
3 cups hot milk
Salt and pepper

Add flour to drippings. On medium heat, cook and stir until flour begins to brown. Add hot milk and stir constantly until thickened. Season with salt and pepper to taste.
Yield: 8 to 10 servings

Roasted Broccoli with Buttered Pecans

4 heads broccoli (cut into large florets)
1/3 cup chopped pecans
1/3 cup unsalted butter or margarine
1/3 cup olive oil
1/2 tablespoon salt
1/3 tablespoon fresh ground
    black pepper

Preheat oven to 450°. In a small saucepan, lightly toast pecans over medium heat. Add butter or margarine, reduce heat to low, and cook until melted. Remove from heat and set aside. Place broccoli in a 9 x 13-inch baking pan. Toss broccoli with oil, salt, and pepper. Bake for 12 to 15 minutes or until browned. Remove from oven. Place in a serving dish. Reheat butter pecan mixture and drizzle over broccoli florets, coating evenly.
Yield: 8 to 10 servings

BELLEVIEW YEAST ROLLS

¼ cup water

1¾ cup milk

5 to 6 cups whole wheat flour

¼ cup instant yeast

1 tablespoon baking powder

3 eggs

⅔ cup sugar, divided in half

1 tablespoon salt

1 stick (½ cup) butter or margarine.

In large bowl, combine water, yeast, half of the sugar, and baking powder. Stir to blend. Set aside to rise while preparing remaining ingredients. In a pan, melt butter or margarine. Add milk and heat until warm (do not boil or overheat). In a medium bowl, combine remaining half of sugar with salt. Mix thoroughly. Set aside. Add flour to the water, yeast, sugar, and baking powder mixture (do not mix). Add eggs, the sugar and salt mixture, and the heated milk mixture. Mix dough to a smooth elastic consistency. Add more flour if needed for desired consistency. Leave dough in the bowl and let rise until it doubles in volume. Punch down dough and cut into desired size for rolls. Place in greased pans (Pam or no-stick cooking spray works best). Place rolls in a warm location and let them double in size again. Bake at 325° to 340° for 6 to 7 minutes. After baking, brush tops with melted butter.

Yield: Approximately 22 rolls

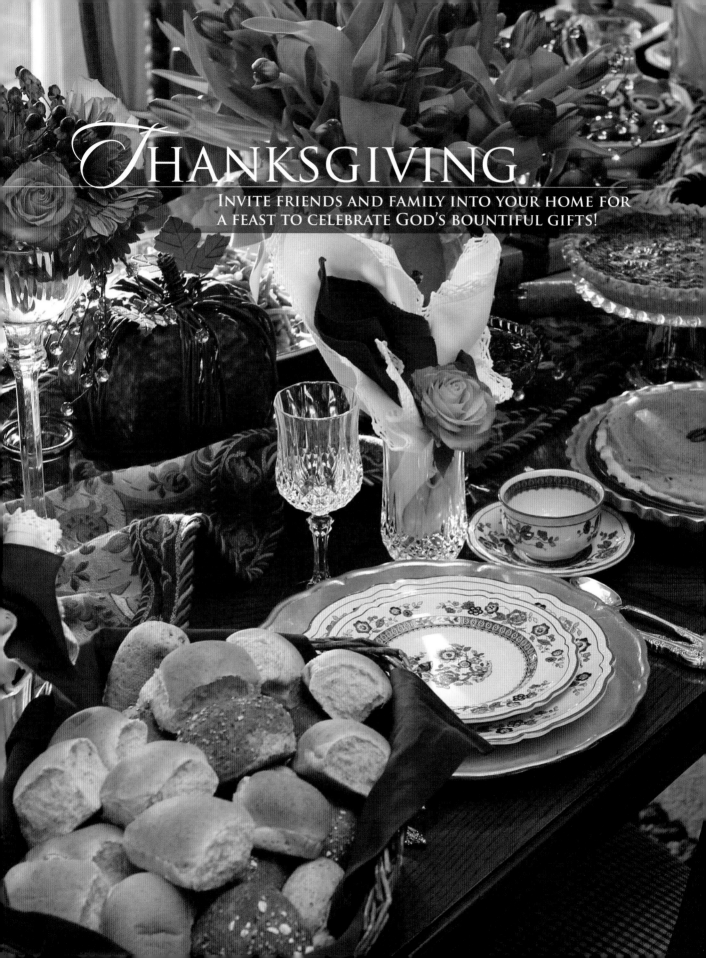

THANKSGIVING

INVITE FRIENDS AND FAMILY INTO YOUR HOME FOR
A FEAST TO CELEBRATE GOD'S BOUNTIFUL GIFTS!

Giving Thanks · *Shirley*

Thanksgiving is a major event in the Dobson home. It begins with a meaningful gathering with relatives who live close by and those who are able to travel. When the big day arrives, excitement, anticipation, and the aroma of roasting turkey fill the air.

When dinnertime is announced, we assemble around the table, and Jim reads a Scripture passage. We all hold hands as he offers a prayer of thanksgiving to God. After we eat the main meal and the table is cleared for dessert, I place three kernels of dried Indian corn beside each plate. I explain that the kernels are to remind us of the first Thanksgiving. After the Pilgrims came to America and endured such a dreadful winter, they made a great feast to

Shirley and her mother, Alma, preparing a holiday meal in the mid-1980s

show gratitude to God for bringing them through. A little basket is then passed around, and as we drop our kernels into the basket, we describe three blessings for which we are most thankful.

Our thoughts invariably turn to loved ones, and we speak with deep feeling and appreciation for each one of them. Usually by the time the basket has circled the table, everyone's eyes are moist from joy and fond remembrances.

We do this every year to thank God for the family He has given us and to reaffirm our need for one another. The tradition becomes more meaningful each year because of the inexorable march of time and its effect on the older ones among us. While some family members are no longer with us, we are grateful for the memories of them, knowing that because of the promise of eternal life, we will see them again. Then we express thankfulness for the new members of our family.

Circumstances continually change, and nothing is constant. But while God grants us breath and life, we will enjoy one another to the fullest and celebrate the love and blessings He has given us.

Come, let us sing for joy to the LORD; let us shout aloud to the Rock of our salvation. Let us come before him with thanksgiving. PSALM 95:1-2

Let's Gather 'Round the Table · *Danae*

Each year at this time, our loved ones come together to rejoice in our blessings and relish in bountiful feasts of mashed potatoes and gravy, buttery rolls, dressing, and cranberry sauce along with other foods that follow family tradition. A golden, oversized turkey rests strategically at Dad's end of the table. The scene is reminiscent of the famous Thanksgiving painting by Norman Rockwell. It represents our version of an American tradition, and we love it.

I am a bit embarrassed to tell you that my grandparents were very exclusive about this celebration. They rarely invited outsiders to join us at the table. I'm not sure why, but it was strictly a family affair. Fortunately that tradition began to change on my parents' watch.

I'll never forget the time my friend Dan joined us for Thanksgiving. One week earlier he had mentioned that he wasn't going to make it to Idaho to be with his family, so I invited him to our celebration. I must admit that I was a little reluctant, given the fact that Dan didn't know any of my family members and I wasn't sure how it was all going to play out. But as you might have guessed, Dan's presence turned out to be a blessing for him and for my family.

That afternoon when it came time to pass our traditional basket around the table and express gratitude for our blessings, Dan was especially touched. Tears welled in his eyes as he conveyed how much it meant to him to share Thanksgiving with us. He expressed gratitude to the Lord and to us for allowing him to be part of such a meaningful day. Dan's tearful response came as a surprise to me because I had no idea he had a tender spirit.

Since that day my friend has relocated to Idaho. He and I keep in touch, and when Thanksgiving rolls around, he often reflects on the time he spent with us. I'm glad my family and I could give Dan that special memory. It's a healthy reminder about how small acts of love can make a big difference in someone's life.

Give thanks to the LORD, for he is good.

PSALM 118:1

Shirley's recipe box.

Menu

Turkey

Mashed Potatoes and Gravy

Peas

Beans or Asparagus with
   Slivered Almonds

Rolls

Black Olives and Sweet Pickles

Cranberry Sauce

Aunt Lela's Marvelous Stuffing

Tossed Green Salad with
   Aunt Lela's Salad Dressing

Candied Sweet Potatoes

Shirley's Traditional Pumpkin
   Chiffon Pie

Pecan Pie

Apple Pie

AUNT LELA'S MARVELOUS STUFFING

¾ cup enriched cornmeal

1¼ cups all-purpose flour

¼ cup granulated sugar

2 teaspoons baking powder

½ teaspoon salt

1 cup milk

¼ cup vegetable oil

1 egg, beaten

3 eggs

1 pint whole milk

½ loaf white bread (no heels)

1½ cups chopped celery

1 cup chopped yellow onions

1 medium yellow onion, grated

Turkey drippings

Salt and pepper to taste

Heat oven to 400º. Grease a 9 x 13-inch baking pan. In a large bowl, combine enriched cornmeal, flour, granulated sugar, baking powder, and salt. Stir in the milk, oil, and 1 beaten egg, mixing just until dry ingredients are moist. Pour batter into the prepared pan. Bake at 400º for 20 to 25 minutes or until light golden brown and a wooden pick inserted into the center comes out clean. Cool, crumble,

and set aside. Crumble ½ loaf white bread on a cookie sheet. Bake at 400° until lightly toasted. Allow to cool. In a large skillet, sauté chopped onions and celery in oil until the onions are clear. Mix all ingredients together by tossing gently, not stirring. Add salt and pepper to taste. Mix 3 eggs with one pint milk. Pour into stuffing mixture and toss. Add turkey drippings until mixture is very moist. Add grated onion. Toss well. Scrape into a 9 x 13-inch pan. Bake at 350° for 1½ hours and top is brown. If you have extra uncooked stuffing mixture, bake in another pan.

Yield: 10 to 12 servings (recipe may be doubled for larger group)

AUNT LELA'S SALAD DRESSING

    1 cup mayonnaise
    ½ to ¾ cup ketchup
    Granulated sugar to taste
    Vinegar to taste

In a small bowl, combine mayonnaise and ketchup. Whisk with a hand whip until well blended. Add small amounts of vinegar and sugar to your liking. If too thick, add a small amount of water.
Yield: 8 servings

CANDIED SWEET POTATOES

    1 large (2 pound, 8 ounces) and
        1 small (1 pound, 13 ounces)
        cans yams
    2 tablespoons cornstarch
    3 to 4 handfuls golden brown sugar
    1 teaspoon cinnamon
    ½ teaspoon nutmeg
    Butter or margarine
    ½ cup chopped pecans
    Marshmallows

In a measuring cup, pour ½ cup yam juice and set aside. In a medium bowl, combine 1½ cups yam juice with cornstarch. Whisk until lumps are gone. Pour into sauce pan and bring to a boil. Simmer, stirring constantly until thickened. Place all yams (without juice) in a casserole dish, cutting large yams in half. Pour cooked juice over yams (continue reserving the ½ cup juice that was set aside). Add brown sugar, cinnamon, nutmeg, and pecans. Stir thoroughly. Dot butter or margarine on top. Bake uncovered at 325° for 20 to 30 minutes. Check yams while they're cooking. If juice appears too thick, add a portion of reserved yam juice. Five minutes before yams are done, place marshmallows on top. Toast lightly.
Yield: Approximately 10 servings

Shirley's Traditional Pumpkin Chiffon Pie

1 baked 9-inch pie shell
1 tablespoon (1 envelope) unflavored
    gelatin
¼ cup water
1½ cups pumpkin
1 cup golden brown sugar, packed
½ cup milk
3 eggs, divided
½ teaspoon salt
1 teaspoon pumpkin pie spice
4 tablespoons granulated sugar
Fresh whipped cream, a sprinkle of
    nutmeg, and chopped pecans for garnish

*Mix together gelatin and cold water. Set aside
for 5 minutes. In the top of a double boiler, mix
together the pumpkin, brown sugar, milk, egg
yolks, salt, and pumpkin pie spice. Cook over
the boiling water in the lower half of the double
boiler for 10 minutes, stirring constantly until
thick. After mixture has cooked for 10 minutes
or so, add gelatin. Stir until dissolved. Chill
until mixture begins to set. In a medium bowl,
gradually beat the 3 egg whites. Slowly add
4 tablespoons granulated sugar, 1 at a time.
Beat until soft peaks form. Fold meringue into
chilled pumpkin mixture. Pour into baked pie
shell. Chill until set. Garnish with fresh whipped
cream, nutmeg, and chopped pecans.*
Yield: 1 (9-inch) pie

Winter

CHRISTMAS

KEEP THE FOCUS ON THE REASON FOR THE SEASON BY
BUILDING MEANINGFUL TRADITIONS WITHIN YOUR FAMILY.

CHRISTMAS AT THE DOBSONS' · *Shirley*

Christmas has grown so commercialized that it's hard to keep the focus on the true meaning of the celebration—even in a house of faith. So, when our children were still young, Jim and I started traditions to help us keep the birth of Christ at the center of Christmas, and they have continued to this day.

Every Christmas Eve family and friends sit down to a wonderful meal together. Afterward we gather around the fireplace as Jim reads the story of Christ's birth from the Bible (Luke 2). Then we dim the lights, and I give each person a votive candle. As the candles begin to glow, I explain that Jesus is the Light of the world who came to bring hope and eternal life to His followers (John 8:12). Then we take turns describing blessings for which we're thankful and sharing something we are asking God to do in our lives in the coming year. After that we blow out our candles, and Jim closes in prayer.

On Christmas morning we open the small gifts in our stockings before enjoying the traditional Dobson Christmas brunch of cinnamon rolls, scrambled eggs, orange juice, and coffee. After brunch we sit around the tree, and one of us plays Santa by passing out gifts. We open them one at a time so we can preserve the happy moment as long as possible.

Danae and Ryan opening gifts on Christmas morning, 1975

Our traditions aren't unique, but they are meaningful. They emphasize two vital themes of the Christmas story—the celebration of Jesus' birth and life and the celebration of love for one another and for the entire human family.

For to us a child is born, to us a son is given, and the government will be on his shoulders. And he will be called Wonderful Counselor, Mighty God, Everlasting Father, Prince of Peace.

ISAIAH 9:6

I once heard a father describe a typical Christmas morning in his household. He said his children always got up early in the morning and hurried to the tree to tear into their presents. They went through them as fast as they could, not stopping to express appreciation for their gifts. They tossed them aside and grabbed for more. The father said that watching that depressing scene left him feeling like a materialistic enabler. Consequently his boys and girls missed the true meaning of Christ's birthday.

My mom shared with you how she and my dad tried to keep the focus on the true meaning of Christmas when my brother and I were growing up. Yes, there were toys and visits to Santa, but we never lost sight of the real reason for the season. Our parents made certain of that.

My friend Karen has done the same. As a mother of six, she prioritizes the birth of Christ for her family. One of the ways she does this is by setting up a nativity scene in early December and purposely leaving the manger empty. Then on Christmas morning, one of her children is given a special package to open. It has the baby Jesus inside. That child places Jesus in the manger as the family sings "Happy Birthday" to the King of kings!

Another great tradition was described in an article I once read. The writer shared that when Christmas is over, and it comes time to toss the tree (a sad

thought, I know), her father chops off two pieces of the trunk and saves them until Easter. When the season arrives, he nails the pieces together to form a cross and drives them into the backyard lawn. The cross stands to remind his family of the connection between Christ's birth and His resurrection.

The Dobsons have our own meaningful Christmas traditions, as my mom described. Each one is carried out in a spirit of joy for that blessed event when Jesus came to this earth as a tiny baby to save us from our sins. It is because of that great act of love that we celebrate Christmas and Easter in their seasons. The friends, food, and festivities that surround our holidays are an expression of praise to God for "his indescribable gift" (2 Corinthians 9:15).

I'm grateful to my parents for never losing sight of Christ's birth, death, and resurrection.

But seek first his kingdom and his righteousness, and all these things will be given to you as well. Matthew 6:33

Pork Tenderloin with Cranberry-
    Apricot Glaze
Cheese Almond Rice Casserole
Creamed Peas
Cranberry Molded Salad
Miniature Herb Rolls
Pecan Pie
Holiday Delight (beverage)

PORK TENDERLOIN WITH CRANBERRY-APRICOT GLAZE

1 large (14-ounce) pork tenderloin
3 tablespoons olive oil
⅓ cup chopped dried apricots
⅓ cup craisins

RUB MIX

2 teaspoons fresh rosemary, chopped
1 teaspoon ground cumin
1 tablespoon ground garlic
½ teaspoon cinnamon
¼ teaspoon salt

Preheat oven to 400°. Rub the pork with the rub mix. Heat olive oil in a large skillet over high heat. Add pork and brown all sides for about 5 minutes. Transfer meat to cutting board and slice the pork lengthwise ¾ of the way through. Fill with chopped apricots and craisins. Tie together with cotton string. Transfer to roasting pan. Roast until thermometer registers 155° (about 25 minutes). Let the pork rest for 25 minutes. Slice pork into medallions and drizzle with remaining pan sauces.

CHEESE ALMOND RICE CASSEROLE

- 1 cup uncooked white rice
- 2 tablespoons minced onion
- ¼ cup minced parsley
- ½ cup sliced almonds
- 1 (4-ounce) can mushrooms with stems
- 1 (14-ounce) can condensed chicken bouillon or consommé
- 1 tablespoon margarine
- 1 pound sharp cheddar cheese, grated

Combine all ingredients except cheese in a sauce pan and bring to a boil, stirring well. Pour into greased 1½-quart casserole dish. Cover tightly and bake at 375° for 30 minutes. Uncover and gently stir in the cheese with a fork. Continue baking uncovered for 15 minutes.
Yield: 6 to 8 servings

CRANBERRY MOLDED SALAD

- 2 small (3-ounce) packages strawberry Jell-O
- 2 cups water
- 1 cup smooth (not jellied) cranberry sauce
- 2 medium oranges, crushed
- 1 sweet apple, medium, finely chopped
- 1 small (8-ounce) can crushed pineapple
- 1 cup finely chopped walnuts

Make Jell-O according to instructions on the package. Allow to sit until liquid becomes the consistency of syrup. In a small pan, melt cranberry sauce on low heat. Add to Jell-O. Stir in all other ingredients. Spray a Jell-O mold with cooking spray. Pour mixture into mold. Place in refrigerator until set.
Yield: 8 servings

Miniature Herb Rolls

¼ cup butter or margarine
1½ teaspoons chopped parsley
½ teaspoon dill seed
3 tablespoons Parmesan cheese
1 package refrigerator biscuits

Place butter, parsley, dill seed, and cheese into a metal 9–inch pie pan. Stir and melt the mixture over low heat. Cut each biscuit into quarters and swish each piece in butter mixture. Arrange pieces so they touch. Bake uncovered at 425° for 12 to 15 minutes.
Yield: 4 to 6 servings

Holiday Delight

2 quarts apple juice
2 quarts cranberry juice
Spice ball filled with mulling spices
Sugar to taste
1 jar maraschino cherries with stems,
    drained

In a large pan, combine juices and spice ball. Steep for up to 3 hours on low heat. Add sugar to taste. Pour small amount of beverage in bottom of narrow fluted glasses. Add one maraschino cherry to each glass. Place glasses in freezer. Chill the rest of beverage in refrigerator. Before serving, pour remaining chilled beverage into glasses.
Yield: 16 servings

Inviting a Guest for Christmas

Bring joy to someone in need by including that person in your Christmas celebration.

Jim's dad, James Dobson Sr., died three weeks before Christmas after suffering a massive heart attack in September. It was a devastating loss for our little family but especially for Jim's mom, Myrtle. We will always regret not having that last Christmas season with Jim's father, which would have been filled with love and laughter, children, and wonderful food from my mother-in-law's kitchen. Instead we struggled to cope with our loss. Three things sustained us during that time: the love of one another, the support from caring friends, and the precious promise of eternal life.

Having been through this experience, I am even more aware that Christmas can be an especially lonely time for those who do not have family nearby. As members of the body of Christ, we must be willing to open our homes and hearts to people in need.

That is precisely what we did one Christmas Eve when we invited an elderly woman who needed a loving family to join us. Her name was Mamie Hendricks. She was in her eighties and the widow of a missionary. Mamie bubbled over with joy when we asked her to join us. At the dinner table that evening, she was the center of attention. All the conversation focused on this wonderful lady as she shared her experiences with us.

After dinner Mamie opened several scrapbooks she had brought. Apparently no one had been willing to look at them for years, but there was meaning for her on every page. She told us about her deceased husband and how much she loved him. She described her life on the mission field and talked about the people they had introduced to the Lord. Then she talked about her husband's death and how she missed him. Story after story poured out. Our two children sat enthralled as they listened to Mamie's recollections of a lifetime.

We had thought that evening with our friend would be our gift to her, but Mamie contributed much more to each of us. She is gone now, but I cherish that evening we spent together.

As we all look toward our holiday plans, may I encourage you to invite a lonely person, someone who is older, or a single adult to join you? I believe you will recognize that it is, indeed, "more blessed to give than to receive" (Acts 20:35).

Therefore, as we have opportunity, let us do good to all people, especially to those who belong to the family of believers.
GALATIANS 6:10

95

Menu

Chicken and Rice with Festive Garnish
Holiday Hot Fruit Salad
Rolls
Spinach and Artichoke Delight
Eggnog Cake
Christmas Apple Cider

CHICKEN AND RICE WITH FESTIVE GARNISH

6 chicken breasts
¼ cup rice, uncooked
1 (10¾-ounce) can cream of chicken soup
1 (10¾-ounce) can cream of celery soup
1 (10¾-ounce) can cream of mushroom soup
¼ cup butter or margarine, melted
¼ cup French dressing
¼ cup milk
1 cup carrots, thinly sliced
Parmesan cheese
Fresh parsley leaves for garnish

Pour rice into greased 9 x 13–inch baking pan. Mix the soups, butter or margarine, French dressing, and milk. Pour half of mixture into the pan with rice and stir thoroughly. Place chicken pieces on top. Pour the rest of the mixture on top of the chicken. Sprinkle carrots evenly throughout the pan. Top with Parmesan cheese. Bake at 275° for 2½ hours. Remove from the oven and garnish with parsley leaves.
Yield: 6 servings

HOLIDAY HOT FRUIT SALAD

1 (15.25-ounce) can sliced pears
1 (15.25-ounce) can sliced peaches
1 (15.25-ounce) can peeled and halved apricots
¾ (20-ounce) can chunk pineapple
2 bananas
1 cup golden brown sugar
1 teaspoon curry powder
⅓ cup butter or margarine
1 small bottle maraschino cherries

Drain canned fruits overnight in a colander. Arrange in baking dish with apricots on top. In small saucepan, heat brown sugar, curry powder, and butter or margarine. Pour over fruit and bake uncovered at 325° for 1 hour. Just before serving, slice a banana and stir into the fruit (optional).
Yield: 6 to 8 servings

Spinach and Artichoke Delight

2 (10-ounce) packages frozen, chopped spinach
1 (8-ounce) package frozen or 1 (14-ounce) can artichoke hearts
1 (8-ounce) package cream cheese, softened
½ stick butter, softened
2 teaspoons lemon juice
Salt and pepper to taste
Bread crumbs
Parmesan cheese

Cook and drain spinach. In large bowl, combine cream cheese, butter, and lemon juice. Beat with an electric mixer until smooth. Add spinach and seasonings. Place layer of quartered, drained artichokes in 10 x 6-inch buttered baking dish. Cover with spinach mixture. Top with bread crumbs and Parmesan cheese. Bake at 350° for 20 minutes (until bubbly).
Yield: 6 to 8 servings

Eggnog Cake

1 yellow cake mix
1 (3.4-ounce) package instant vanilla pudding
4 eggs
1 cup oil
1 cup dry sherry or cooking wine
2 tablespoons nutmeg

In a large bowl, combine all ingredients and mix at medium speed for 3 minutes. Spray a Bundt pan with no-stick cooking spray. Pour mixture into pan. Bake at 350° for 50 minutes or until a wooden toothpick inserted into the center comes out clean. Place the large circular cake on a silver platter and put holly and red berries around it to make it look like a wreath. Dust lightly with powdered sugar to give the illusion that the wreath has snow on it.
Yield: 8 servings

Christmas Apple Cider

½ gallon apple cider
1 quart cranberry juice
1 large (12-ounce) can frozen lemonade (undiluted)
5 whole cinnamon sticks
1 teaspoon whole cloves
½ teaspoon allspice
¼ cup golden brown sugar (optional)

In a large pan, combine all ingredients and place on low heat. Bring to a boil. Simmer for 5 minutes. Remove from heat and strain. Put spices in a tea ball and put back into cider (optional). To use a 20-cup coffee pot to heat the cider, pour the cider, juice, and lemonade into the coffee pot as you would water to make coffee. Place the spices in the basket. Serve hot.
Yield: Approximately 20 servings

New Year's Day

Ease into the new year with a relaxed day of watching football and indulging in traditional Southern fare.

My dad's favorite holiday is New Year's Day. He loves the relaxed atmosphere combined with our traditional foods and one football game after another. If the University of Southern California happens to be in a bowl game, so much the better! (My dad is a former professor and alumnus.)

My mom and I love New Year's Day too. After the hustle and bustle of the Christmas season and staying up past midnight to ring in a new year, we welcome the opportunity to kick back and unwind. We put on our jeans or sweatpants and fall back on the sofa to watch the Rose Parade and the Rose Bowl Game. It's not uncommon for us to nod off a time or two in between it all. Who could blame us?

The best part of the day is our traditional lunch of Southern red beans and ham over rice with hush puppies. It might seem a bit odd to those who aren't accustomed to it, but this meal is something we look forward to all year. The recipes were handed down by my grandmother, Myrtle Dobson (affectionately known to me as Myrna), who was a fabulous cook. We serve her cornbread hush puppies piping hot with butter and honey just like she did, and they're delicious! Her Southern red beans are equally as tasty, especially when sprinkled with chopped green onions and a drizzle of Tabasco. A tossed green salad with avocado completes the meal and everyone goes back for second helpings. Did I mention the hot apple pie à la mode? It's not hard to figure out why we need to fall back on the sofa after all that good food!

In our family New Year's Eve is celebrated in a more formal fashion. On that night we get dressed up and dine at a fancy steak house with friends to reflect on the past twelve months and anticipate what lies ahead. Later everyone heads to our house to toast one another with sparkling cider as we watch the famous ball drop in Times Square. We never part ways before my dad leads our group in prayer. He asks God to bless us during the new year and watch over our comings and goings. I appreciate the fact that he makes prayer a priority, because it's fitting that we should put the Lord first on such an occasion.

If you're like me, watching the clock roll into a new year is exciting but a bit unnerving too. Maybe that's why hearing the tune "Auld Lang Syne" stirs up an uneasy feeling for me. I think it reflects fear of the unknown—another new year, another blank canvas, not knowing what's going to transpire or if anything catastrophic will occur. When those thoughts come to mind, I focus my attention on the One who's in command. What a comfort to know that He not only sees the future, He owns it! We can step boldly into January first with the assurance that He has absolute power and authority over everything. We can be at peace knowing He's in complete control.

For this God is our God for ever and ever; he will be our guide even to the end.

Psalm 48:14

Menu

Grandmother Myrna's Southern Red Beans and Ham over Rice
Grandmother Myrna's Southern Hush Puppies
Tossed Green Salad with Avocado
Hot Apple Pie a là Mode

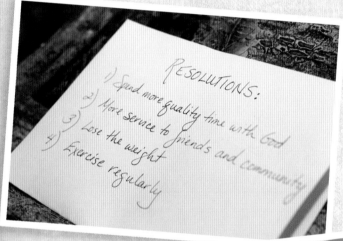

GRANDMOTHER MYRNA'S SOUTHERN RED BEANS AND HAM OVER RICE

1 (16-ounce) package pinto beans
1 small precooked ham, fat removed and
    cut into pieces
White rice (We recommend converted
    long grain white rice.)

The night before, sort beans and remove small rocks and bad beans. Rinse beans thoroughly under running water. Pour beans into a very large pot and add enough water to cover beans (approximately 3 inches). Soak overnight. Before cooking, rinse beans again and cover with fresh water (approximately 3 inches). Bring to a boil. Reduce heat to medium low. Cover with lid. Check on beans frequently while cooking. Lift them occasionally from bottom of pan with large spoon (don't stir). After beans have cooked 2 hours, add ham and salt to taste. Add more water if necessary. Cook for approximately 2 to 3 more hours until beans are tender and juice has thickened (keep them uncovered for the last hour so they will cook down). Prepare rice according to package directions for the quantity needed. To serve, ladle beans over rice.
Yield: 12 to 15 servings

GRANDMOTHER MYRNA'S SOUTHERN HUSH PUPPIES

2 cups white cornmeal

½ cup grated yellow onion

1 tablespoon granulated sugar

1 teaspoon salt

⅛ teaspoon baking powder

½ stick (¼ cup) butter or margarine at room temperature

1 cup plus 1 to 2 tablespoons boiling water

1 pan of cold water for dipping hands

In a large bowl, combine cornmeal, sugar, salt, and baking powder. Make a well (hole) in the center of cornmeal mixture. Place butter or margarine in the well. Boil the water and pour all but approximately 2 tablespoons of water over margarine. Stir mixture to moisten. If needed, gradually add 1 to 2 tablespoons remaining boiling water to create a mush consistency. Add grated onions. Mix together with spoon. Dip hands in pan of cold water and then take a small amount of mixture and mold into a 2-inch oblong shape. Continue shaping dough until all the mixture is gone. Fill large frying pan 1 inch deep with oil. When oil begins to gently bubble, test temperature by dropping in a small piece of white bread. If the bread floats and quickly turns golden brown, the oil is ready. Deep fry each hush puppy until golden brown. Remove when done, set on paper towels, and blot excess oil. Serve immediately with butter or margarine and honey (optional).
Yield: Approximately 15 hush puppies

Valentine's Day

CELEBRATE THE DAY OF LOVE WITH A FESTIVE ALL-RED DINNER.

From the Heart · *Danae*

My mother has always made Valentine's Day special. As a child I could count on coming home from school to find her preparing an all-red meal with exception to the bread. Spaghetti was often on the menu along with pink lemonade, red Jell-O, and cherry pie or cobbler. We would eat together as a family and present one another with cards and "sweet nothing" gifts as tokens of our love.

As an adult I've continued this tradition of creating an all-red dinner on Valentine's Day. When I'm unable to celebrate with my family in Colorado, I enjoy cooking a meal for friends. Some of my favorite recipes include healthy turkey meatloaf in red sauce, heart-shaped rolls with red sprinkles, and my hint-o'-pink mashed potatoes. By "hint" I mean using a tiny drop of red food coloring to create the slightest hue of pastel pink. My friend Carrie wanted to copy this idea for her family on Valentine's Day, but she made the mistake of using too much red dye. Her mashed potatoes were fuchsia in color, and her family refused to eat them. A hint of pink is about all anyone can tolerate, including me.

One recipe that is always a hit with guests is my Aunt Lela's warm cherry cobbler with cherry chip ice cream. I use a heart-shaped cookie cutter to make an indention on the top crust and then fill it with pink and red sprinkles. It looks pretty atop the counter or on the living room server when guests arrive.

For Valentine's Day decorations, I tie heart-shaped balloons on the back of guests' chairs and use white plates and pink cloth napkins. Long tapered candles with a fresh floral arrangement provide a nice centerpiece, and I can find affordable flowers at the grocery store. After my tabletop is finished, I place a Valentine's Day card and a wrapped heart-shaped chocolate by each guest's place setting. (We all need a little chocolate on Valentine's Day, don't we?) Sometimes I sprinkle heart-shaped confetti in the center of the table for a touch of sparkle.

It's fun to be creative on Valentine's Day and provide a warm memory for family and friends, but the love we have for God and for one another is the main priority. You might want to emphasize this to your guests during the meal. If you have children, Valentine's Day is the perfect time to talk about the two greatest commandments that Jesus taught us: "Love the Lord your God with all your heart and with all your soul and with all your mind" and "love your neighbor as yourself" (Matthew 22:37,39).

Valentine for Grandfather Jim

The concept of love was God's idea, and in fact, the Bible defines Him as being love (1 John 4:8). Our Valentine's Day cards, candy, and flowers are a celebration of His gift to us.

For as high as the heavens are above the earth, so great is his love for those who fear him. PSALM 103:11

A TIME FOR ROMANCE · *Shirley*

*V*alentine's Day is one of my favorite times of the year. Unfortunately, sometimes it's hard to convince men of that day's special nature. It took time to convince my husband, Jim, how important this holiday can be. In fact some of you may remember his description (or confession) about our first Valentine's Day from one of his newsletters.

> February 14 is Valentine's Day. Despite its commercial underpinnings, I think this celebration is a great idea. Men need all the help they can get in remembering that their wives are incurable romantics. I certainly do.
>
> I had trouble understanding Shirley's romantic nature when we were newlyweds. On our first Valentine's Day, I had spent ten hours poring over books and journals in the USC library. I had forgotten the date, and even worse, I was oblivious to the preparations going on at home.
>
> Shirley had cooked a wonderful dinner, baked a pink, heart-shaped cake with 'Happy Valentine's Day' on top, placed red candles on the table, wrapped a small gift, and written me a love note. The stage was set for her to meet me at the front door with a kiss and a hug. But I sat in a library across town, unaware of the gathering storm.
>
> When I put my key in the lock about 10 p.m., I knew something was horribly wrong. The apartment was almost dark—and deathly quiet. A coagulated dinner was still on the table, and half-burned candles stood cold and dark in their holders. It appeared that I had forgotten something important. Then I noticed the red-and-white decorations. *Oh, no!* I thought. There I stood, feeling like a creep. I didn't even have a valentine, much less a thoughtful gift for Shirley.
>
> Fortunately, Shirley is not only a romantic lady but a forgiving one. We talked about my thoughtlessness later that night and came to an understanding. I learned a big lesson about Valentine's Day and determined to never forget it.
>
> It is never too late to put a little excitement into your relationship. Romantic love is the fuel that powers the female engine. Remember, men, marriages must be nurtured or they can wither like a plant without water. And wives should recall that when a woman believes in her husband and respects him, he gains the confidence necessary to live responsibly.

After reading this commentary, one woman asked how I taught my husband the importance of romantic occasions, including the real meaning of Valentine's Day. It was a good question. Jim will tell you today that he was attuned to my needs in those early years because I was so supportive of him. He said I believed in him before he believed in himself. He is a brilliant man, and I have always been proud to be on his team. In turn my respect for Jim has made him want to understand me and meet my needs.

If you will honor your husband, he may want to know what matters to you. It doesn't always work that way, but it certainly did in my marriage. And it wouldn't hurt to drop a hint or two a week before the special occasion.

My command is this: Love each other as I have loved you. John 15:12

HEALTHY TURKEY MEAT LOAF IN RED SAUCE

1 pound ground turkey

3 egg whites

18 saltine crackers

¼ cup oatmeal, uncooked

3 tablespoons oat bran

1 cup canned peas and carrots

⅓ cup canned corn

2 tablespoons Worcestershire sauce

1 clove garlic, minced

¼ teaspoon pepper

SAUCE

1 (6-ounce) can tomato sauce

½ white onion, finely chopped (optional)

2 tablespoons golden brown sugar

Dash Worcestershire sauce

2 tablespoons chopped fresh parsley
    for garnish

In a large bowl, with your hands combine ground turkey, egg whites, crackers, oatmeal, oat bran, peas and carrots, corn, Worcestershire sauce, garlic, and pepper. Spray a medium roasting pan with cooking spray. Place portion of meat mixture on a cutting board. Flatten so meat is approximately 1-inch thick. Press down firmly with a medium-sized, heart-shaped cookie cutter. Place heart-shaped meat loaf in roasting pan. Continue until all meat is used. Bake at 350° for approximately 20 minutes.

To make the sauce, combine tomato paste, brown sugar, onions (optional), and Worcestershire sauce in a small sauce pan. Mix together and cook on medium heat. Serve as gravy over meat loafs. Garnish with parsley. Yield: 4 to 6 servings

CANDIED CARROTS

4 carrots, sliced
Equal parts honey and maple syrup
Sesame seeds
1 drop red food coloring
Dash of salt and pepper

*Steam carrots until almost done. Add salt and
pepper. In a separate pan, combine honey and
maple syrup and bring to a boil. Add carrots
and coat well. Add sesame seeds and red food
coloring. Stir gently. Remove from heat and
serve immediately.*
Yield: 8 servings

CINNAMON APPLESAUCE MOLDED JELL-O

½ cup red cinnamon candy pieces
2 cups boiling water
2 small (3-ounce) packages lemon
    Jell-O
2 cups smooth applesauce
3 (3-ounce) packages cream cheese
¼ cup light cream
2 tablespoons mayonnaise
½ cup walnuts, chopped

*Dissolve candy in boiling water. Add
Jell-O and stir to dissolve. Stir in
applesauce. Chill until mixture begins
to thicken. Spray an 8 x 8-inch pan
with no-stick cooking spray. Pour
Jell-O mixture into pan. In a medium
bowl, combine cream cheese, cream, and
mayonnaise. Spoon on top of gelatin and
swirl to create marble effect. Sprinkle
chopped walnuts on top. Chill for 8 hours
until firm.*
Yield: 9 servings

AUNT LELA'S CHERRY COBBLER

2 (14.5-ounce) cans red tart cherries
    in juice
1½ to 2 cups sugar
1 teaspoon cinnamon
1 handful all-purpose flour
Butter or margarine
Unbaked pie crust

*Pour cherries and juice into an 8 x 8-inch
or 8 x 10-inch baking dish. Add sugar
and cinnamon. Sprinkle flour on top and
smooth with hand. Dot with butter and
set pie crust on top. Bake at 425° for
1 hour, checking cobbler after 40 minutes.*
Yield: 8 servings

CELEBRATE WINTER GAME NIGHT

IF THE WEATHER OUTSIDE IS FRIGHTFUL,
THAT'S A GREAT TIME TO BUILD A FIRE AND
ROUND UP THE TROOPS FOR A GAME NIGHT.

GAME PLAN · *Danae*

*W*henever I visited my Grandma Alma and Grandpa Joe as a child, I could count on homemade meals and dozens of table games. Some of our favorites were Aggravation, Uno, and Yahtzee. We played for hours. Grandpa Joe was a fierce competitor who loved to win more than anyone I've ever known. Winning was fun for me too, but for Grandpa Joe it was a passion. Even when he was ninety years old, he still reveled in getting the best of me.

Grandma Alma was a serious competitor too. Whenever we played Aggravation, she used her personal dice because it had a tendency to roll sixes. (I was never able to prove her dice were rigged, although I checked for nicks more than once.) The rules of the game state that a player gets an extra turn if he rolls a six, and it was common for Grandma to toss a string of them. That would enable her to gain a lot of distance around the board, which created nervous energy for Grandpa and me. I can still hear Grandpa complaining about it, but he was too much of a gentleman to turn the board over.

When my parents were with us, we liked to play a card game called "Hearts." Grandpa Joe had played endless games on ships when he was in the navy, and he was very good at it. He beat my dad at Hearts for years without giving any clue about how he was doing it. He would just laugh and say, "Let's play again." Finally my dad cracked the code. When Joe was trying to do something tricky, my dad noticed that his father-in-law's neck would turn red, probably because his blood pressure was rising. Dad would watch for that telltale sign, and when it happened, he knew he was about to be snookered. What a fun memory!

Occasionally I invited a few friends to my grandparents' home for dinner and games. We would bring take-out food and play Hearts all evening. Even though my grandparents were in their late eighties at the time, my thirtysomething friends enjoyed hanging out at their house. They considered my grandparents amusing and fun to be with. My friend Charlie was especially drawn to them. Before moving to another state, he brought a pink rosebush to their home and planted it among their other rosebushes. He wanted it to serve as a reminder of him and his love for them. My grandparents named the rosebush "The Charlie Bush." It still blooms in vivid color each spring.

Danae with Grandpa Joe and Grandma Alma.

My dad wrote about my grandparents in his book, *Bringing Up Boys*. He said:

> I find that children and young people are starved today for family life as it used to be—but almost never is. My in-laws are eighty-nine and ninety years of age, and yet my daughter and her friends love to visit their home. Why? Because everything there is so much fun. They have the time to play, laugh, eat, and talk about whatever interests the young people. Nobody is in a hurry. If they are called on the phone, they are always available to talk. This elderly man and woman, whom I also love, provided something to those who are younger that is simply not available elsewhere. How sad.

Grandpa Joe and Grandma Alma understood the real meaning of hospitality. They have passed on to their eternal home now, and I miss them terribly, but the sound of their laughter and the smell of Grandma's kitchen will always be etched into my mind. And if there are games to be played in heaven, I know Grandpa is giving everyone a run for their money.

Do you and your family have time for game nights? Research has shown that kids who eat dinner with their families have a fifty percent less chance of getting mixed up with drugs, alcohol, and other mischief. The main reason is because dining together invites conversation. Game nights serve that purpose in three ways: kids eat dinner with their parents, they spend quality time together, and they have fun in the process.

The winter season is ideal for board games because families spend more time indoors. Why not build a fire and put a fun buffet together, such as a potato bar with chili or my Grandma Alma's barbecue meatballs (see recipe)? You might ask your children to invite a few friends. Many kids come from broken homes and dysfunctional families, and you can model how a healthy Christian family operates. Even if you're a single parent, you can still provide a dynamic example of what a Christ-centered home is like. As my mom stated in a previous chapter, you'll never know what experiences young people will take with them into later life.

Surely the righteous will never be shaken; they will be remembered forever. PSALM 112:6

Grandma Alma's Busy Day Barbecue Meatballs
Baked Potato Bar with Toppings
Rolls
Grandma Alma's Finely Chopped Salad
Popcorn
S'mores

GRANDMA ALMA'S BUSY DAY BARBECUE MEATBALLS

1½ pounds ground beef
1 egg, slightly beaten
½ cup Ritz crackers
1 teaspoon salt
Dash of black pepper

SAUCE

1 cup ketchup
2 tablespoons golden brown sugar
1 tablespoon Worcestershire sauce
1 tablespoon vinegar
½ teaspoon salt
Dash of black pepper
½ cup minced yellow onion

In a large bowl, combine beef, egg, crackers, salt, and pepper. Mix thoroughly with your hands. Shape into medium-sized balls. Place in a frying pan on medium heat. Brown both sides. Place in a baking dish. In a medium bowl, combine ketchup, brown sugar, Worcestershire sauce, vinegar, salt, pepper, and onion. Mix and pour over meatballs. Bake at 350° for 1 hour.
Yield: 8 to 10 servings

GRANDMA ALMA'S FINELY CHOPPED SALAD

Iceberg lettuce
Radishes
Green onions
1 tomato
1 ripe avocado

Slice lettuce into thin shreds. Finely chop radishes and green onions. Cut avocado and tomato into chunks. In a salad bowl, combine vegetables and serve with Italian dressing.

Seasoned
Hostesses

Seasoned Hostesses

We now come to the final entry in this book. Since we've been talking about the significance of hospitality, I thought it would be encouraging to hear from some other women (besides my wonderful mom) who are veterans at putting this gift into practice. Granted there are many who could have contributed a great deal of wisdom and insight, but after making this a matter of prayer, the Lord laid the following three ladies on my heart. They share a common denominator—each has weathered challenges of biblical proportion and has chosen to remain strong in her faith. Despite loss, heartache, and unanswered questions, they've continued to press on and use their gifts and talents to bless others.

Last month I conducted phone interviews with these women individually and recorded their responses. Our conversations were filled with laughter, tears, and gratitude for what God has accomplished! As you will see from reading their testimonies, each of these dear ladies is, indeed, an inspiration.

Danae

Rosa Gialloreti
Clinton Township, Michigan

DANAE: Rosa, I had the privilege of getting acquainted with you this year, and I could really sense the love of Christ radiating through your personality. When your friends told me that you were somewhat of a "hospitality guru," I said, "I need to find out more about this lady!" It's been a blessing to hear what God is accomplishing through your ministry.

ROSA: Thank you. I came to know the Lord later in life, so I understand the difference between living a life with Christ and without Him. Before becoming a Christian, nothing satisfied me. I always felt a void. But now I have peace, even in the midst of trying, painful circumstances.

DANAE: You're obviously speaking from experience. Describe what you went through.

ROSA: Six years ago I lost my husband to cancer. Before he became ill, we had a very good life. I loved him, and he was my "rock." After he died I was overwhelmed with grief and cried for months! It was during the worst of my pain that I wound up in the hospital. Fortunately I had the support of Christian friends who loved and cared about me. They came to the hospital to pray for me, and God provided a healing. Now I have extraordinary strength! I'm so active, and I know it's because of Him. It's a miracle, considering that I couldn't even move from a chair for a period of time.

DANAE: I'm so sorry you went through such a trauma. How did you work through your grief?

ROSA: Friends would quote Jeremiah 29:11, which speaks about God's plan to give me a hope and a future. I would say, "Well, this doesn't feel like a good plan to me." But I kept going through the motions. I went to Bible studies when I didn't want to, I stayed active in my church, and I invited people over when I was lonely. I kept reaching out even though I didn't feel joy. I would pray, "*Lord, bring back my joy!*" For a long time I couldn't concentrate, but I kept doing and working. Now when I hear people say in their distress, "I don't know what to do," I tell them, "Just do *something*—even if it's serving coffee. Force yourself to be with Christian people and serve in a small way, and God will open a door."

DANAE: After your husband passed away, you didn't feel like entertaining for a long time. When did you begin opening your home again?

ROSA: I gradually developed an ability to have people over. I started by creating a place in my basement to hang out with girlfriends. As I grew stronger, I invited those who were in need or hurting to come over and have a dish of pasta. From there women of all ages from my church started coming to my home to share skills.

DANAE: Now you do quite a bit of entertaining, don't you?

ROSA: Yes. I love to exercise my gift of hospitality! In the past I used my gift to bless my husband, but now my ministry has expanded. When I feel lonely, I'll say to myself, *Okay, I'll have a dinner party, or a girls' spa night, or I'll have a few girls over to do some cooking*.

DANAE: What does your girls' spa night entail? I love that idea!

ROSA: I invite three women to my home for an evening of massages, manicures, pedicures, and facials. There are a couple of ladies at my church who own a spa business, and they perform the services for us. I play Christian music and make spa-type food, such as wraps, salads, and chocolate-covered strawberries. The gals stay overnight, and we have breakfast together. It's great therapy for a mom who needs to get away or a friend who's going through a difficult time. Some of the women whom I invite are not Christians, and it gives me an opportunity to talk about the Lord in front of them.

DANAE: What are some other ways that you use your gift?

ROSA: I enjoy bringing couples together to encourage them over food. One time I called my pastor and his wife and asked, "Who would you like to have dinner with?" They mentioned a couple they wanted to get to know better, so I called them. I had never met these people, but I invited them for dinner and told them that my pastor and his wife would be there and I'd love to meet them. We ended up having a wonderful time of fellowship. That's what I like to do. If I see new people at church whom I think might share an interest with some others I know, I'll invite them over. They get acquainted with one another, and we have a blast. It's one form of uniting the body of believers.

DANAE: I know you've also helped others who were grieving by having them in your home. How did you minister to their needs?

ROSA: I attended a grief share course and found it to be so helpful that I decided to become a facilitator. Twelve people from my church met at my home every Monday night for eighteen weeks. Each of us had lost someone, so we were all in the same boat. During the first few weeks, the people were so grief stricken, but after a while I saw their countenances begin to change as we moved through the course. We prayed together and shared what God was revealing to us. I have to say that the Lord showed up at that class every week! His presence was always there.

DANAE: I'm not surprised because Scripture tells us, "The Lord is close to the brokenhearted." It must have been a blessing for you to help those who were going through the same kind of suffering you experienced. Did you cook comfort foods for them?

ROSA: Yes. I made dinner every week, and I tried to cook healthy foods that I thought they would enjoy. I loved shopping and making different recipes and filling the table. It made me feel good when they raved about the meals. I wasn't able to cook for my husband anymore, but this group of people loved my food and was so complimentary. It made me want to cook more. After the class ended, one of the girls told me that the food that I served every week was one of the highlights—it made her feel welcome.

DANAE: How do you use your talents in your church?

ROSA: I'm the banquet coordinator, and I help facilitate women's conferences.

I also teach cooking classes, which is something my pastor's wife encouraged me to do. I started teaching women how to make pretzels, and then later I rallied them into my home to make pretzels for the food pantry at church, which is a ministry that caters to families in need. Last December we made six hundred pretzels! Our church also has a fund-raising event for missions, so a group of gals and I got together to make bonbons, chocolate-covered strawberries, and pretzels to sell at the event. Before the night was over, every pastry was gone! God has really expanded my borders. I started doing dinner parties, and now it's become a ministry to the masses.

DANAE: Rosa, you have quite the gift of hospitality!

ROSA: I hear that a lot. Initially when I took a spiritual gifts test and discovered my gift was hospitality, I wasn't happy. I wanted to have something more profound. I thought hospitality was only about working in the kitchen. But then I began to understand all that it entails—nurturing, loving, caring, making people feel welcome. It's a very important role, and it took time for me to realize that.

DANAE: You're exactly right, and that's why my mom and I have written this book! Any tips to pass along?

ROSA: If you're having friends over, do everything ahead of time so you can enjoy the evening. For instance when I see chicken on sale, I'll buy ten pounds, clean it up, and put it in my freezer. I'll also make pastas ahead of time, such as lasagna rolls or stuffed shells and freeze them. In the winter when I have people over, it's easy for me to pull out my chicken and pasta and make a nice salad. Another thing I would suggest is not to be afraid to let your guests help. They love to be part of things! Let the men barbecue. Above all have fun. Set the atmosphere with music, candles, and flowers. Create warmth and love in your home.

DANAE: Great advice! I'm thankful that you seem to be doing so much better. You've come a long way!

ROSA: Grief is a process that cannot be rushed. I still miss my husband terribly! He came to know Christ before he died, so I know I'll see him again. In the meantime, I'll keep encouraging and comforting people in the way God has done for me. I've been able to take everything that He's contributed to my life and turn it around to share with others. I can truly say that my joy has returned.

CLARITA GUSTAFSON
Arcadia, California

DANAE: Through the years you've opened your home to many friends and family members on a variety of occasions. What motivates you to do that?

CLARITA: My desire to be hospitable is born out of my love for people. Whether it's a club that one of my children belongs to, a church organization, or a neighborhood or community event, I enjoy sharing my God-given talents. I find it very fulfilling. Also I love to celebrate everything! I have get-togethers for all our national holidays, friends' milestone birthdays, and even simple occasions, such as a friend's first trip to Paris.

DANAE: I've seen you "work the room" during your parties to make sure everyone is engaged and included. You'll say, "Danae, do you know Sharon?" or "Have you met Lisa?" Explain how you're able to do that while overseeing all the details that go with being a hostess.

CLARITA: I don't allow myself to become distracted. It would be easy for me to get caught up with guests I know on an intimate level and forget to practice the real gift of hospitality, which is to bring newcomers into my circle. I try to keep an eye on my guests so I know everyone is enjoying themselves. As the little social clusters emerge, I move from group to group. I make sure no one is standing alone.

DANAE: You often invite people from different walks of life to your parties—singles, those who are going through difficulties, people of various ethnic origins, and even nonbelievers. Where did you come up with that idea?

CLARITA: I grew up seeing my parents incorporate many different types of people into their social circle. My parents were very hospitable—that's how they expressed love to others. When I'm planning an event, I often pray over my guest list.

DANAE: I've noticed that when it comes time to get everyone's attention before the meal is served, you honor the Lord first and then your husband, Darryl. You refer to him as your hero and your "braveheart." I can tell by the expression on his face that he appreciates it, even though he's embarrassed. Explain the little ritual that you do.

CLARITA: As I ring my silver bell to welcome my guests, the first person I acknowledge is the Lord Jesus Christ. Then I express appreciation to my husband for giving me moral support in putting the event together. I say it with great enthusiasm and from the bottom of my heart. I would encourage all wives to do that, regardless of whether their husbands made a minimum or large contribution toward the event. By doing so, you're honoring Christ.

DANAE: Some of your relatives and friends are nonbelievers. When they're at your parties, how do you deal with that challenge?

CLARITA: Christ is the head of our household, so He gets recognized at each event. The main way we do that is by praying before meals. It doesn't matter what type of group it is—whether it's our granddaughter's soccer team or a community event. As the hostess, I ask if we may say a blessing. I also acknowledge Christ in front of people in my home. I try to be sensitive and not overbearing about my faith, but I'm not inhibited. For example when I have girlfriends from my gym class over (we call ourselves "The Divas"), two-thirds of them are not Christians. I express my views, but in a spirit of love and respect.

DANAE: You obviously feel very comfortable around nonbelievers.

CLARITA: I never mind having unsaved people in my home because it provides an opportunity for me to express love and appreciation for them. Once I've established more intimate relationships, I begin planting "seeds" to win them to the Lord.

DANAE: At your annual Christmas party, you and your husband emphasize the reason for the season. I appreciate the fact that you bring Christ into your celebration.

CLARITA: We invite both believers and nonbelievers, and we make it very clear that our Christmas party will be in honor of Jesus' birthday. People know what to expect, and we leave it up to them to decide if they'd like to come. During the party as I ring my bell to get everyone's attention, I use that opportunity to acknowledge Jesus. Then I take a few moments to recognize our guests before turning it over to my husband who leads us in prayer. Following dinner everyone moves to the living room where a friend plays the piano and leads us in singing Christmas carols.

DANAE: How do your unsaved family members respond to the sing-along?

CLARITA: Very favorably. In fact for the past several years, some of them have asked to come to our home on Christmas Eve, which is one of our more religious celebrations. Before the gifts are opened, everyone gathers around Darryl as he reads the entire story of Jesus' birth from the book of Luke. It's interesting that one of our relatives, an atheist, prefers to sit next to Darryl for the reading.

DANAE: As an experienced hostess with many years practicing hospitality, what advice would you give?

CLARITA: Reach out to both Christian and non-Christian friends and incorporate them into your social circle. Also you need to find a balance for yourself. I often think of the story of Martha and Mary, which illustrates the practice of hospitality (Luke 10). Martha became distracted by all the preparations of the meal and was annoyed with her sister for sitting with Jesus and not helping her. Jesus did not reprimand Martha when He said, "Mary has chosen what is better." I must admit that's one area where I've erred in the past. There have been times when I've had an event coming up and chosen not to decline other offers of commitment. I've wound up feeling overwhelmed. It's hard to say no, but I'm getting better at bringing a sense of balance to my life.

DANAE: Twenty years ago you and your family went through a devastating experience when you lost your four-year-old son, Aaron, to leukemia. What was the greatest lesson God taught you through your grief?

CLARITA: To lean on Him exclusively! I cannot emphasize that word "exclusively" enough. Before Aaron became ill, I understood a certain dependence on the Lord, but through his death I learned to be completely dependent. I came to know and to feel the power of the Holy Spirit in a way I had not experienced before.

DANAE: What did you do to cope during that time?

CLARITA: I never took my focus off the Lord. I remained steadfast and became immersed in His Word. Job became one of my most significant characters in Scripture. I would often recite his words in Job 1:21, "The LORD gave and the LORD has taken away; may the name of the LORD be praised." I also quoted Jesus' words to His Father on the Mount of Olives as He was preparing to go to the cross, "Yet not my will but yours be done."

DANAE: Were you ever angry at God?

CLARITA: There were times during my angry sessions when I would argue with the Lord in my prayers and ask why. As parents there's something within us that tells us we should go before our children. But I came to realize that Jesus died before His mother, and the ultimate sacrifice He made for me on the cross overrides any form of suffering I could experience.

DANAE: When did you begin to open your home again?

CLARITA: We lost Aaron in October, and I felt compelled to reach out to people soon after that. I still had my Thanksgiving celebration that year, which was a family affair, and I went ahead with my annual Christmas party and had a large gathering. I encouraged myself to use my son's home-going as an opportunity to reach out to others and glorify God.

DANAE: And now, twenty years later?

CLARITA: Aaron is the catalyst for sharing the gospel. When nonbelievers come to my home, they see photos of him in every room. That's when I say, "Only because of my faith in Jesus Christ—my anchor and my refuge."

SHERRI MARTIN

Destin, Florida

DANAE: When I think of you, the Proverbs 31 woman comes to mind. I know you've always had a heart for the home. What contributed to that?

SHERRI: When I was young, I pored through the Scriptures to try to figure out what we as women are called to do. I kept seeing a common thread that related to the vital role we have to play in the home. Not that we can't be successful in other areas, but the Bible places great emphasis on our responsibility to show love to our husband and children, to watch over the affairs of our household, and to be hospitable. I've always viewed my home as a place where my family gathers to regain strength. For that reason I've tried to create a warm and loving environment, so when the front door closes, our home becomes our sanctuary.

DANAE: Given your love for your family, how devastating it must have been for you to see your marriage fall apart. What were the circumstances?

SHERRI: I was thirty-two when my husband walked out on me and our three children. I had enjoyed being married and loved my husband dearly. I couldn't understand how he could break his vows and abandon our family. My only hope was in Christ. He was faithful to carry me and the children every step of the way.

DANAE: How did you manage to hold your family together in the midst of that crisis?

SHERRI: After my husband deserted us, I was essentially a widow, and my children were orphans. The Bible talks about how God takes care of widows and orphans, so I was certain He would provide for us. The question was how were we going to take care of others? I told my kids, "We may not have much, but we're going to share what we have." I asked them to collect all their money and bring it to me. (The children were two, six, and ten.) They put all their pennies on the table. I said, "This money belongs to God." I went on to tell them that everything under our roof was owned by Him. He was the center of every aspect of our lives, including our home life.

DANAE: How long were you a single mom?

SHERRI: Fifteen years. During that era, I poured all my energy into my children, my church, and my work. I carried three jobs, and the main reason why I took the third job was so we could afford to have people over. I wanted my children to see hospitality in effect. I also felt a responsibility for them to be able to have their friends over. I told my kids, "We're going to give the very best to our family and friends. If we're invited somewhere, such as a dinner event at church, we will bring the highest quality food that we can afford and make it look as attractive as possible."

DANAE: How were you able to work three jobs and be a hands-on mom?

SHERRI: The Lord helped me to be available, although I wish I could have been in the home more while my kids were growing up. I taught Sunday school, and I was always willing to open my door. When my kids were teenagers, their friends confided in me when they were going through difficulties. I would give advice and pray with them. Now that they're young adults with families of their own, they still call me and say, "I need your help."

DANAE: You've since married a wonderful Christian man named Rod. I know he's been a tremendous source of strength and support for you. I wish I could say it's been happily ever after, but the two of you have weathered some rough storms, literally. Describe what you went through.

SHERRI: Rod and I moved to Florida in 2004, and within a few months, Hurricane Ivan destroyed our home. We were out of town, so we weren't able to save any of our belongings. All the hospitality items that I had collected through the years were gone. I was literally digging through mud trying to find things.

DANAE: How did you cope with losing your home and possessions?

SHERRI: I was down emotionally, but I'd been through tough times before. I clung to the memory of how the Lord provided for my needs and gave me new ministry in each trial from the past. Even though the hurricane wiped out family photos and other cherished items that could not be replaced, I knew God would supply what He wanted me to have. Speaking of which, the first gift that Rod and I received to restore our library was a set of autographed books from your dad. That meant so much to us! We love to tell that story, and people cry when they hear it.

DANAE: I remember when my dad sent that gift to you. I'm glad his books were used by the Lord to bless you during that dark time. Unfortunately your troubles didn't end there, did they?

SHERRI: No. Less than two years after the hurricane occurred, I found out I had cancer. It was a fast growing tumor that required surgery, chemotherapy, and radiation. I stayed in bed for twelve months and saw very few people. I couldn't cook and was unable to eat most of the food that friends wanted to bring. It was a wilderness journey—a period when God slowed me down and gave me a lot of time to think and pray.

DANAE: What was going through your mind during that season of uncertainty?

SHERRI: People used to ask me how I was dealing with being sick and not knowing if I would survive. I told them that regardless of what happened, I was going to be okay. I lay in bed thinking of ways that I could serve others if God chose to heal me. I wanted to be like Peter's mother-in-law in Matthew chapter eight. Scripture tells us that she was sick for a period of time, but after being healed, she immediately got up and began to wait on her guests.

DANAE: You have a true servant's heart, Sherri. How is your health now?

SHERRI: It's been five years since my illness, and I feel wonderful. God has been gracious to allow me to live. My cancer was one small moment in eternity.

DANAE: And how are you doing in the aftermath of losing your home?

SHERRI: The material things that were destroyed during the hurricane were exactly that—things! God gave me what I needed. My husband and I built a new home, and we've been living there for a year. It has beautiful views, and the setting is perfect for entertaining. Picture this. I have shiny copper pots hanging from my kitchen ceiling and every gadget you can imagine! The Lord replenished what I lost far above what I dreamed possible.

DANAE: That is characteristic of the nature of God! What are some ways you've taken His blessing and turned it around to bring glory to Him?

SHERRI: Rod and I wanted to give our home a name, and we decided to call it "Grace Hall." We told the workmen involved in our building project how God had been so gracious to us and that our home was a gift from Him. They marveled and said, "That makes us want to work harder!" Before Grace Hall was finished, we had a hard hat party for fifty friends. My husband stood in front of everyone and talked about the story of Job from the Bible. He explained how God had restored to Job what had been taken from him. Then my husband related that to me and said that once again God had shown mercy in bringing restoration.

DANAE: It is, indeed, amazing to consider all the ways the Lord has brought beauty out of ashes in your life, Sherri. Your new home is one more testimony to His faithfulness!

SHERRI: It truly is. However, Rod and I have accepted that God could take this home from us too. It belongs to Him, and He can do whatever He wants with it. But while we're living there, we will practice hospitality to bless others. Last Thanksgiving we had twenty-five guests, and everyone enjoyed a time of prayer and singing from special hymnals that we ordered for the house. Each hymnal has "Grace Hall" printed on the front cover.

DANAE: That's really neat. What are some other ways that your home has been used to minister to people?

SHERRI: We've hosted retreats for many groups, including elders from our church and teens involved with youth ministry. Last December we opened our home to two hundred and fifty people for a charity fund-raiser. I had three Christmas trees and greenery everywhere. It looked like an old-fashioned Christmas! Guests commented, "You must have been collecting these items for years!" I laughed and replied, "More like five minutes!"

DANAE: You have a beautiful spirit, considering all you've been through. How do you maintain a positive attitude?

SHERRI: God's sovereignty covers all the pain that we can't understand. During each of my trials, I've said to Him, "Thank You, Lord, for this difficult time because You're bringing me closer to You. I'm not sure how this situation is going to play out, but I know You love me and You have the perfect plan no matter what." Acknowledging that fact has prevented me from becoming bitter or depressed.

DANAE: Beautifully stated. Any hospitality tips to share?

SHERRI: My advice is to get started. Even if you don't know how to cook very well, it doesn't matter. You can learn. The most important goal is to have the heart and mind of Christ. If you truly believe your life belongs to Him and your home is His possession, you'll want to open your door to people. I often think of when Jesus appeared to His disciples after His resurrection and made breakfast for them (John 21). Jesus was always aware that people were hungry and needy. He not only provided the "bread of life" for them, but He made sure their physical needs were met too.

DANAE: You've done a remarkable job of applying that principle to your life. How would you sum it up?

SHERRI: For me the heart of hospitality is being willing to open my door and ask, "Lord, how can I serve?" I've found that to be the greatest blessing.

I AM MORE CONVINCED THAN EVER THAT GOD INTENDS FOR US, AS BELIEVERS, TO USE THE GIFT OF HOSPITALITY AS A KEY COMPONENT IN FULFILLING THE GREAT COMMISSION. WE ARE CALLED TO REPRESENT JESUS TO OUR WORLD AND HOSPITALITY IS AN EFFECTIVE AND VITAL FORM OF THAT REPRESENTATION. YES, IT IS A HUGE RESPONSIBILITY, BUT ALSO A WONDERFUL OPPORTUNITY. IT IS MY EARNEST PRAYER THAT YOU WILL BE ENCOURAGED AND MOTIVATED TO BE INTENTIONAL ABOUT THE USE OF YOUR HOME TO EXPAND HIS KINGDOM.

Pastor Steve Wingfield

ACKNOWLEDGMENTS

It is a tremendous blessing to be able to share *Welcome to Our Table* with our readers and friends. The concepts, recipes, and personal stories were inspired by many people who have contributed significantly to the creative process. They also came from our personal experiences and our beloved family members, some of whom have gone on to their eternal home.

We are most grateful to the Lord, who blessed us with the opportunity to celebrate His gift of hospitality and share it with others. He placed the idea in our hearts and made it possible to create this book, and now our prayer is that He will use it for His purposes.

A special note of appreciation goes to the hero in our family, James Dobson. We couldn't ask for a more loving and dedicated husband and father. Thank you for your editorial assistance and for taking time away from the office to pose for photos while frying chicken and barbecuing burgers. You're the best!

Wendy Kalina, executive assistant, was invaluable to us in every dimension of this project.

Our good friend Judy Booker worked tirelessly to create the floral arrangements for the spring and summer segments. Thank you, Judy, for sharing your God-given talent and for investing so many hours in this project.

The following three couples graciously allowed us to use their beautiful homes and gardens for the photo shoots: Darryl and Clarita Gustafson, Bob and Judy Booker, and Dr. Fred and Carmen Speirs. We are grateful to each one of you for going the extra mile to provide assistance and even loaning us your china and table decor. What incredible friends you are!

We would also like to express appreciation to our three seasoned hostesses: Rosa Gialloreti, Clarita Gustafson, and Sherri Martin. Thank you for sharing your hearts and your testimonies to the glory of God. Each of you has been a light and an example of what it means to "walk the talk," and we are inspired by your unshakable faith.

The lovely pictures in this book were photographed by Julie Johnson, who caught the vision of what we wanted to convey. Thank you, Julie, for making our recipes and decorations come to life.

Finally, we owe a tremendous debt of gratitude to the folks at Harvest House Publishers for sharing our dream and working with us to make it a reality. Bob Hawkins Jr., LaRae Weikert, Jean Christen, and Peggy Wright poured their time and energy into this project and accommodated us at every turn. It has been a pleasure to partner with you and the rest of your team.